Handmade
SHOES FOR MEN

© 1999 Könemann Verlagsgesellschaft mbH
Bonner Strasse 126, D – 50968 Cologne

Art and Publishing Director: Peter Feierabend

Project Management: Vince Books
Consultancy: László Szőcs
Illustrations: György Olajos
Project Coordination and Editing: Claudia Hammer and Kirsten E. Lehmann
Editor of the original edition: Susanne Kolb
Layout: Gerd Türke, Malzkorn, Cologne
Picture Editor: Monika Bergmann
Production: Mark Voges
Reproductions: Omnia Scanners. Milan

Original title: Herrenschuhe, handgearbeitet

© 1999 for the English edition:
Könemann Verlagsgesellschaft mbH
Bonner Strasse 126, D – 50968 Cologne

Translation from German: Anthea Bell, Terry Moran and Martin Pearce
in association with First Edition Translations Ltd., Cambridge, UK
Editing: Jenny Knight in association with First Edition Translations Ltd.
Typesetting: The Write Idea in association First Edition Translations Ltd.
Project Management: Birgit Dietz for First Edition Translations Ltd., Cambridge, UK
Project Coordination: Nadja Bremse
Production: Ursula Schümer
Printing and Binding: Neue Stalling, Oldenburg

Printed in Germany
ISBN 3-89508-928-1

10 9 8 7 6 5 4 3 2 1

László Vass & Magda Molnár

Handmade
SHOES FOR MEN

Photography Georg Valerius

KÖNEMANN

The more prominent the feet, the more spoiled they are? It has not been proved that all these gentlemen's feet always wear custom-made shoes. Nor do we know from which workshop they might have originated. But shoes are often interpreted as the visiting card of the personality.

Be that as it may, the public appearances of these gentlemen confirm that shoes are the most important things a man wears. They are (from top left to bottom right): Bill Clinton, Clint Eastwood, Michael Hutchence, Sylvester Stallone, Tom Hanks, J.F. Kennedy Jr, Mickey Rourke, Liam Neeson, and Jack Nicholson.

Elegance Begins with the Shoes

Every hand-sewn, custom-made shoe is a precious creation by craftsmen; on the one hand it protects the particularly delicate structure of the human foot from all sorts of unpleasantness; and on the other, as part of the wearer's clothing, it also expresses his taste – and sometimes his position in society as well. Elegance begins with the shoes.

There are two main reasons why people choose to have shoes custom-made for them. One is the thirst for differentiation and individuality: we like to have an influence on everything – the shape, the model, the leather, its color, the combination of different leathers, the thickness of the sole, the height of the heel, the embellishments – for ourselves, so that the shoes will go with a particular suit or be appropriate for a particular occasion. But apart from that, many a man – entirely in line with classical tradition – would like to have an entirely new and modern pair designed for him.

One other reason is rather more prosaic. In general, people arrive in this world with soundly constructed feet, which would serve them well only if they could spend their whole lives walking around barefoot on sandy, stony, or wooded ground. But in our civilized world the feet become accustomed at an early stage to "laziness"; the toddler who is just learning to walk has shoes put on him, and later on this process is encouraged by driving a car, office work, or spending hours in front of the television. But mostly it's the shoes themselves – poor-quality, uncomfortable shoes, that is – that do the most damage. And it is by no means unusual for people that have undergone years of torment to discover, in middle age, that custom-made shoes are the only source of relief.

It is not known exactly when making shoes became a craft, though it was a respected trade in Egypt 4000 years ago. The skills, tricks, and wiles of the craft were refined over the centuries, for until the end of the nineteenth century – when industrial shoe production became widespread – everybody wore handmade shoes or boots.

The shoemaking process today still consists of exactly the same stages as it did 100 or 200 years ago, though today the preparatory stage has undergone a certain degree of specialization, leading to a division of labor. The shoemaker takes the customer's measurements, certainly, but it is the lastmaker who uses these measurements to make the last that takes the place of the foot for the subsequent production stages. The shoemaker selects the leather, but it's the clicker who cuts out the individual pieces and the closer who fits them together; it's real teamwork. When the last with the upper stitched round reaches the workshop, the rules for constructing the shoe are the same as they used to be for both royal shoemakers' establishments and little village workshops.

Making a new pair of shoes is always a challenge to the experience and skill of the shoemaker. From the time the measurements are taken to the moment when the completed, polished shoes are handed over to their future wearer, the shoemaker's eye must not fail him, nor must his hand falter. Even with more than 30 years' familiarity and experience, the "journeyman's sense" of how to produce a masterpiece of a particular model has to be fine tuned from scratch every time. If this process is successful, the saying of Chuang Tse comes true: "If the shoe fits, the foot is forgotten."

This book introduces the skilled craft of making comfortable, beautiful, classic gentlemen's shoes that offer the magic of individuality. In spite of the changes brought about over the centuries by science and technology, to which shoemaking as well as footwear production have not remained immune, the workshops where handmade shoes are produced – whether these are in London, New York, Munich, Vienna, Rome, or Budapest – hold fast with quiet pride to their conservative traditions. These apply in equal measure to the various types of shoe, to the material used, and to the ethics of the profession.

The types of shoe today regarded as classics for the elegant gentleman appeared in the last decades of the nineteenth century. Where the material is concerned, the conservative maxim applies: nothing can replace natural, genuine leather, whether for the upper, the lining, the insole, or the sole. Only leather that has been treated with vegetal tanning agents by a centuries-old technology is selected for these. The sewing thread, too, consists only of the strongest plant fibers, and only natural ingredients are used for the glue.

Step by step the book follows the more than 200 operations that are carried out over a period of some ten weeks to make a single pair of shoes. How can the precise measurements of the foot be determined? What happens in the two years that elapse between the felling of the tree and the emergence of the measurement last? What are the characteristic types and design features of the classic gentleman's shoes? How is the leather for the upper tanned? How about the leather for the sole? Why is the welt the heart of the shoe? Is it worth having handmade shoes repaired? How can we take care of our favorite shoes so that they will last? How does it feel to wear hand-sewn shoes?

Every shoemaker in the world will give more or less the same answers to these questions – even if every workshop, naturally, develops its own special tricks. And they will all be found in this book.

My love and reverence for the shoemaker's craft has helped me to describe everything that goes on day by day in my workshop. With great sensitivity, the photographs portray the various materials, tools, and – not least – the people that create a truly unique product.

My thanks are due to the craftsmen from whom I learned my trade and to those who work for me: their expert knowledge has enabled me to extend my own. Thanks also to Ludwig Könemann, who invited me to write this book.

Special thanks go to my co-author Magda Molnár, who molded the most diverse material into the book you now hold in your hands.

László Vass

It's the little secrets and ruses – some of them closely guarded – of the individual workshops in Vienna, London, or Budapest that make some shoes even better than the best.

Size

Taking the Measurements

No two feet are exactly the same. A shoemaker can only make comfortable shoes of the appropriate size if he is given as much and as precise information as possible about both of the customer's feet. Whereas the tailor producing a custom-made suit recommends two or three fittings, the shoemaker – with the assistance of the so-called trial shoe – must make do with one at the most. This makes it absolutely essential to allow plenty of time for taking the measurements: ideally one or two hours. It often proves difficult to find the right time to achieve the most precise result.

In general circumstances a healthy person's feet are the same size at any time of the day. However, they can be affected by temperature (extreme heat, for example) or by strenuous exercise (walking for a number of hours, or engaging in high-intensity sport). It is therefore recommended that measurements should be taken during the morning.

Then the feet can swell as a result of certain illnesses. If the customer knows that treatment will be completed before long and that his feet will then return to their original dimensions, he should not have his measurements taken until they have done so. However, in the case of a chronic illness, slightly over-sized shoes may make walking easier.

While he is constructing the shoes a shoemaker always takes the greatest possible account of any malformations or pathological changes, such as hammer toes or bunions. But in such cases it may be better, under certain circumstances, for the customer to postpone the purchase of a pair of comfortable shoes until after he has undergone minor orthopedic surgery.

In any case a pedicure is advisable a few days before the measurements are taken in order to avoid problems like ingrown toenails, an inflamed nailbed, or painful corns. Thin, close-fitting socks should be worn so that the measurements will be as accurate as possible.

The taking of measurements is fundamentally a sort of ceremony; it is equally important for it to take place at the right time and to last the right length of time, for any disruptive factors to be eliminated, and for the customer to provide the maximum amount of information. The movements of the shoemaker are almost ritualized, taking place in a predetermined sequence. This ceremony is the basic prerequisite for the preparation of a last that will take the place of the feet as faithfully as possible throughout the production process, and hence for the creation of a pair of shoes that will be a unique work of art.

The shoemaker measures the length, width, height, and circumference of the feet in two different positions: first while they are bearing the weight of the body and again when they are not under strain. In the standing position the foot can be as much as three-eighths of an inch [1 cm] wider, the arch is rather lower, and the tendons and muscles are tense. This position also roughly reflects the state of the feet when they are under strain, that is when walking. But inevitably, shoes stretch – both under the strain of walking and owing to the warmth and moisture of the feet. So if the shoemaker were to treat the measurements taken under strain as "correct," the owner's pleasure in his new shoes – which would be perfectly comfortable from the word go – would in a few short days turn to disappointment when they became too big and loose.

Where measurements are taken in the sitting position the situation is reversed: the feet are smaller when not under strain. Despite this many shoemakers consider these measurements more important, because they constitute a better basis for establishing the varying width of the feet when walking and for estimating the extent to which the shoes will stretch when worn.

The first measurement phase is the visual inspection of the foot to determine its shape. The shoemaker checks whether it is inclined outward or inward with respect to an imaginary axis running lengthwise through the foot,

Measurements are taken in both the standing and sitting positions.

whether the inside arch is high or low, whether the ankle sits lower, whether the heel is strong or weak; he checks the shape of the insteps and the metatarsals and notes the presence of any characteristic malformations (for example flat feet, bunions, protruding little toes, big toes higher than usual, hammer toes). To do this the shoemaker needs to feel the feet all over, sensing their shape and outline with his hands. He observes the customer's gait, which may be substantially affected by his body weight or by unconscious mannerisms. Some people are light on their feet, while others cannot walk without stamping – and this is why the shoemaker also examines with great care the shoes that the customer was wearing when he came, for the way these are misshapen (whether they lean one way or the other, at what points the soles and heels are worn) may provide indications that will be useful when making the new pair.

The shoemaker then has a discussion with his customer. Generally very few people have any idea of the condition of their feet. The most they will say is that "shoes always pinch my big toe" or "all shoes are tight over my insteps." This indirectly brings up more information that is important for the size and shape of the new shoes. For example, people suffering from diabetes or constricted arteries must not wear tight

The shoemaker establishes the shape of his customer's feet by touch.

footwear: their shoes must be made slightly looser. Such considerations are, of course, crucial in the design and making of a person's shoe. A perfect fit is the desire of both customer and shoemaker. A gentleman needs to be able to put his trust in the team responsible for providing him with his shoes, and it is in the shop's interests to produce the best shoes for him so that he will come back for more and recommend the service to his friends.

The various stages of shoemaking can be seen in this shoemaker's workshop, among them the use of a foot gauge to take measurements (right). This copperplate print, one of a series entitled "Craftsmen's workshops with their principal implements and processes," was made in Esslingen in 1836. It is interesting to observe the footwear of the craftsmen.

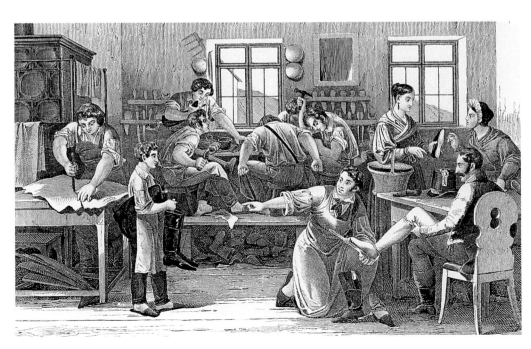

The Draft

There's a golden rule among shoemakers: the simpler the measuring device, the more reliable the measurements. Even the most exclusive workshops make do with two shoe heels, two sheets of paper, a shoemaker's tape measure, a right-angled bracket, a pencil, a device for measuring the length of the foot, as well as the requisite items for making a sole imprint (indigo paper or a footprint measure).

In order to determine the length and width of the new shoes, drafts – outlines of the feet – must be drawn. The pencil must be exactly vertical to the paper when this is done. If it were to lean outward away from the foot (this is also called "underdrawing"), the result would be shoes at least one size too small. The shoemaker draws the line from the heel, along the inside of the foot to the big toe, round the tips of the toes, and back along the outside of the foot to the heel. The toes are pressed down during this process so that they extend to their full length. As the left and right feet are never absolutely identical, the process is repeated with the other foot.

Once the draft has been taken the shoemaker marks the location of the first and fifth toe-joint bones (see page 19) and the outermost points of the outer and inner metatarsals and of the heel, so as to prepare for the actual measurement of the foot.

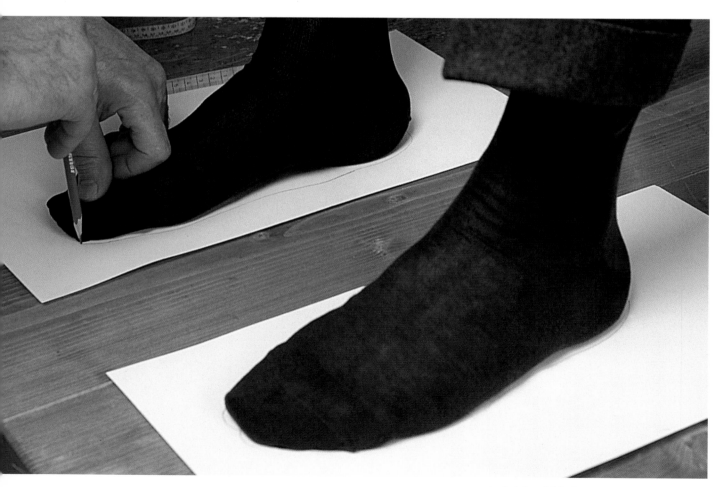

As the left and right feet are never absolutely identical, drafts of both feet must be taken.

The Length and Width of the Foot

The length and width of the foot can be measured from the draft with a special shoemaker's tape measure. This consists of a nonelastic textile strip calibrated differently on each side.

One side of the tape measure, which is calibrated in numbers of stitches, is used to read off the length of the foot. Traditionally the French stitch-measurement system is used, in which one division is equal to about a quarter of an inch [6.667 mm]. The shoemaker then increases the result by one and a half; if the foot is measured as 41, for example, the fitting itself should be 42.5 – because the foot generally stretches by about three-eighths of an inch [1cm] when walking. The shoes would not be comfortable when walking if the toes were jammed against the toecaps and the feet had insufficient room for movement.

The other side of the tape measure is marked in metric units – centimeters and millimeters. This side is used to measure the widest point of the foot – that is the distance between the inner and outer metatarsals – on the basis of the points marked on the outline.

These measurements are then checked with the Brannock gauge, which has the scale divisions for length and width marked on its plate. The foot is placed on the device and the heel firmly pressed into the heel cup, and the shoemaker then reads off the foot length from the scale. Two freely moving slides – one moving horizontally, the other vertically – are then used to determine the width of the foot.

The Bannock gauge allows for an accurate measurement of foot size and is an indispensable tool in the shoemaker's workshop. There are different gauges available for different countries, but each performs essentially the same function. Customers worldwide have reason to be thankful to the Bannock gauge for their foot comfort.

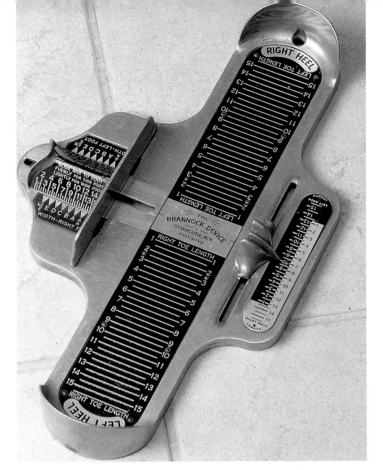

This Brannock gauge is used to check the shoe size and width number (see page 26). The scale on this one shows English sizes.

The foot must be placed on the device with the heel against the heel cup, and the toes pressed onto the base. The shoe size can then be read off correctly.

The shoemaker's tape measure has different scales on each side: one gives the length of the foot in French sizes (in which one division equals about a quarter of an inch [6.667 mm]), while the other gives the width of the foot in the metric system, that is in centimeters and millimeters.

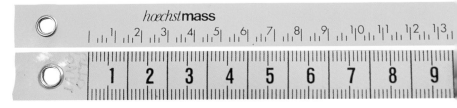

The Foot Imprint

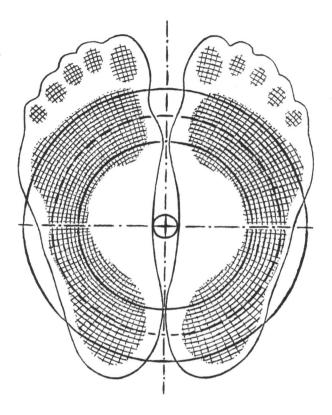

When placed close together the feet form a dome-like curve.

After the draft, the imprint; this is taken with a Ped-a-graph that provides an accurate picture of the condition of the arches, and enables both the intersection points of the arch curves and the location of the toes to be determined.

A rubber membrane with one side densely covered in pimples is painted with ink and laid on a sheet of paper with the painted side downward. The foot imprint is taken in a sitting position. The customer puts a little weight on the foot being measured, which transfers the ink to the paper, the color being darkest where the load is greatest. The lastmaker will make sure that the sole of the last is slightly elevated at points corresponding to the darker patches.

An arch with an ideal shape in both the longitudinal and transverse planes leaves hardly any traces. If the entire surface of the sole leaves colored traces, this is an indication of one of the most common malformations of the feet: fallen arches.

This problem can be successfully treated at an early stage with well-made, comfortable shoes containing inserts to raise the arches. So it is important for the shoemaker to get an accurate picture of the state of his customer's arches.

The foot imprint is taken with the Ped-a-graph.

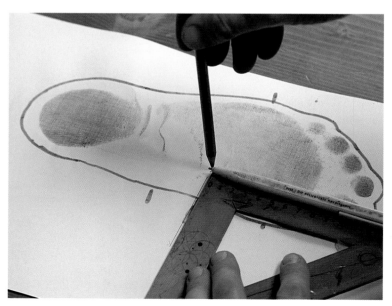

The line linking the big toe and the heel determines the actual length of the foot.

The Foot from Different Angles

The side elevation provides further important information about the shape of the foot. The foot is placed on the measuring sheet with a heel piece underneath it of the same height as the new shoes; this puts the foot in the correct position. A drawing board is set up alongside the foot and the side view traced onto the paper. This drawing shows the height of the toes, the rise of the instep, and the bow of the heel. The heel elevation is also very useful, for example in determining the width of the heel and deciding on the shoe type. The shoemaker obtains additional information by measuring the height of the ankle, which affects the height and shape of the uppers.

With the knowledge obtained from the draft, the imprint, the various elevations of the foot, and its critical points, the shoemaker marks up the areas where it diverges from the norm on a prefabricated blank that will be fashioned into the last. Of course, there is no such thing as a "normal foot", and it would be surprising if there were no deviation from the dimensions of the blank.

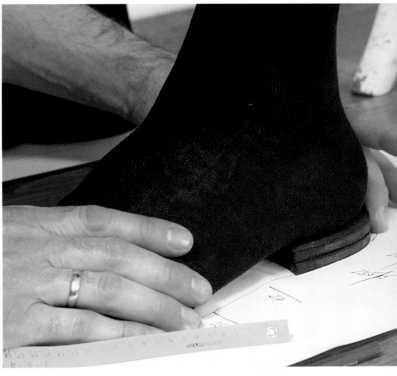

A heel piece is placed under the heel to bring the foot into the correct position.

The side elevation shows the height of the toes and of the instep.

This elevation indicates the shape of the heel.

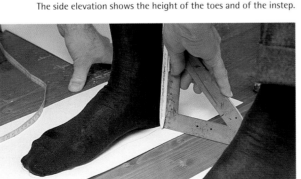

The height of the ankle is important for shoes as well as boots.

The shoemaker rechecks all the measurements (the blank last is on the right).

The Bone Structure of the Foot

From the origins of the shoemaker's craft in ancient times until the end of the eighteenth century, shoemakers practicing their trade concentrated exclusively on the external shape of the foot for which they were to provide a protective covering, utterly ignoring what lay beneath it: the bone structure and musculature. Not until the nineteenth century did master craftsmen realize that a shoemaker simply cannot do without a knowledge of anatomy. Numerous shoemaker's primers appeared, summarizing the essence of the shoemaker's craft – most of them beginning with a description of the anatomical characteristics of the foot.

Today a study of the characteristics of the bone structure, the musculature, the joints, the tendons, and also the skin of the foot is part of the standard training in the shoemaker's craft. The taking of measurements is based on anatomical fixed points selected in accordance with rules formulated over decades of practice. These points are characteristic and easy to recognize, and they manifest only small variations when measurements are taken repeatedly.

Although it is true that no two feet are absolutely the same, their anatomical structure is identical in every human being. This structure first appeared some two million years ago, when for reasons still disputed to this day the progenitor of modern man – *homo erectus* – stood upright and began to walk on two legs.

Of the 208–214 bones in the skeleton the ones to be found in the most mobile parts of the body, the hands and feet, are among, the smallest. The bones, joints, muscles, and tendons of the foot jointly constitute the most complex mechanical structure in the human body. The area of the soles of the feet totals less than 46 square inches [300 sq. cm], yet when standing they must reliably bear an average body weight (for men) of between 150 and 260 pounds [70 and 120 kg], and when walking they adapt flexibly to any surface unevenness. The soles of our feet make delicate internal adjustments to enable us to walk barefoot in the soft, shifting sands of a seaside beach, and to negotiate rough, stony paths.

The foot is thus an extraordinarily resilient structure that is capable of amazing achievements. According to an English study the average central European covers 93,000 miles [150,000 km] on foot during his lifetime. The case for comfortable shoes could not be better made.

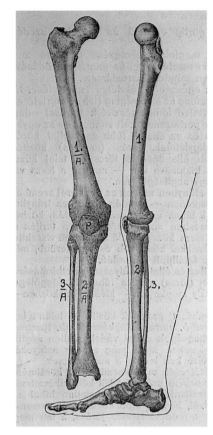

The shoemaker's primer by József Bodh published in Budapest in 1920 contained anatomical illustrations appropriate to the standards of the period.

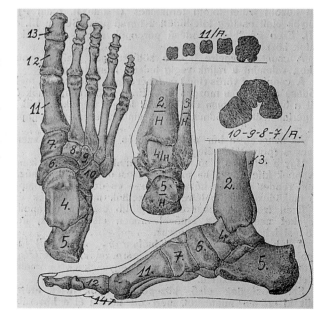

A
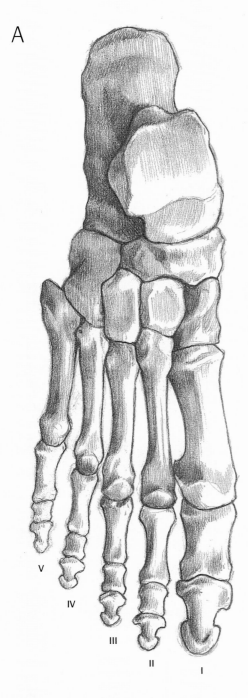

V

IV

III

II

I

B
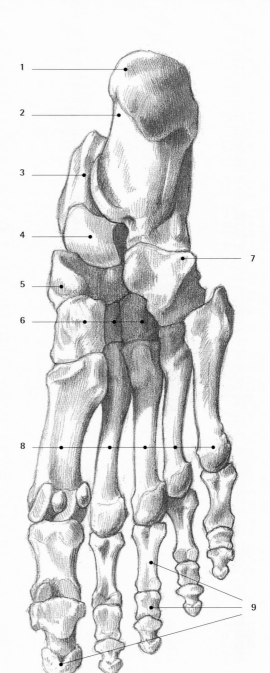

1

2

3

4

5

6

7

8

9

These views of the 26 bones of the foot, as seen from above (A) and below (B), show that the seven tarsal bones (items 1–7) are the most highly developed, because they bear the greater part of the body weight. It is clear from figure A that the length of the foot is equal to the distance between the end of the heel bone and the tip of the big toe, while its width is determined by the five metatarsal bones (8). The thickest of these metatarsal bones is that of the big toe; that of the second toe, the longest; and that of the little toe (V), the shortest. Toes II–V consist of three phalanges, while the longest and widest toe, the big toe (I), has only two phalanges.

1. Body of heel bone (tuber calcanei)
2. Heel bone (calcaneus)
3. Ankle bone (talus)
4. Ankle-bone head (caput tali)
5. Navicular bone (os naviculare)
6. Cuneiform bones (ossa cuneiformia)
7. Cuboid (os cuboideum)
8. Metatarsal bones (ossa metatarsalia)
9. Toe bones (digiti pedis)

The Musculature of the Foot

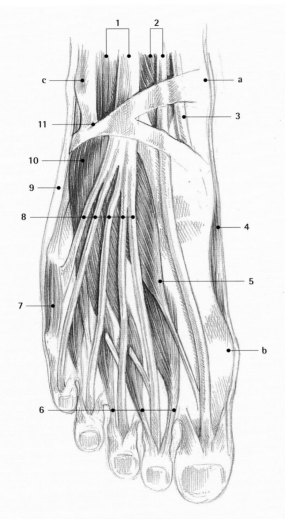

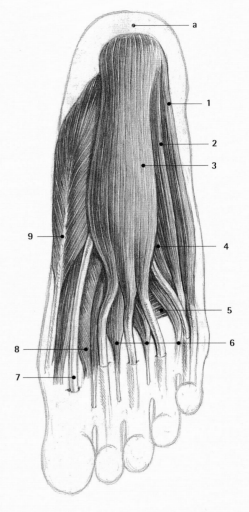

The musculature of the foot as seen from above
1. long toe extensor (m. extensor digitorum longus)
2. long big-toe extensor (m. extensor digiti I longus)
3. shinbone-muscle tendon (tendo m. tibialis anterior)
4. big-toe spreader (m. abductor digiti I)
5. short big-toe spreader (m. abductor digiti I brevis)
6. interosseous muscles of the instep (three) (mm. interossei dorsales)
7. small toe spreader (m. abductor digiti V)
8. tendons of the long toe extensor (tendo m. extensor digitorum longus)
9. fibular-muscle tendon (tendo m. peroneus tertius)
10. short toe extensor (m. extensor digitorum brevis)
11. inferior transverse tendon-retaining ligament (ligamentum cuboideonaviculare dorsale)
a inner ankle bone (malleolus medialis)
b phalanx of the proximal big-toe joint (articulatio metatarso phalangea)
c outer ankle bone (malleolus medialis)

The musculature of the foot as seen from below
1. little-toe spreader (m. abductor digiti V)
2. little-toe bender (m. flexor digiti V)
3. short toe bender (m. flexores digitorum brevis)
4. interosseous muscles of the sole (four) (mm. interossei plantares)
5. big-toe adductor, transverse head (m. adductor digiti I, transverse head)
6. "vermiform" muscles of toes II–V (mm. lumbricales digitorum II–V)
7. tendon of the long big-toe bender (tendo m. flexor digiti I)
8. short big-toe bender (m. flexor digiti I brevis)
9. big-toe spreader (m. abductor digiti I)
a heel bone (calcaneus)

The bones form the foot's load-bearing structure, while the muscles, which are attached to the bones with tendons, carry out its movements. Muscles generally operate in groups rather than singly. A single movement of the body – taking a step forward, for example – can involve several muscles, some of them acting in opposite directions. All the muscles of the foot are small and short, their function being to support the musculature of the lower leg – some by bending, some by stretching. The spaces between the metatarsal bones are occupied by small muscles whose function is to spread the toes apart or draw them together. In comparison with the fingers, though, the movements of the toes are very limited. The small muscles of the soles of the feet play an important part in maintaining the arches. Beneath the thick skin of the soles and the fatty tissue underlying it there is a strong band of muscle whose function is to protect the nerves and blood vessels within.

The foot has an unusually large and complex network of blood vessels and nerves. The nerve fibers transmit the impulses that trigger muscle contractions. They send the brain a continuous stream of information about the position of the limbs and the posture of the body, and they also transmit any sense of pain.

The skin of the soles functions both as protection and as a receiver of stimuli. It is resistant to elastic, mechanical strain (pressure, for example), and the chemically acidic secretion from its glands forms a protective barrier against pathogens. The soles of the feet are especially rich in sweat glands, with some 2300 to the square inch [360 to the sq. cm]. The volume of perspiration they produce can be substantial. People tending to perspire heavily should take care to avoid footwear containing synthetics; naturally breathing leather counteracts fungal infections and bacterial complaints. Some people find their feet sweating causes more discomfort than perspiration from any other part of the body, and have to wash their feet frequently. Perhaps this unfortunate situation would be alleviated if their shoes were a better fit.

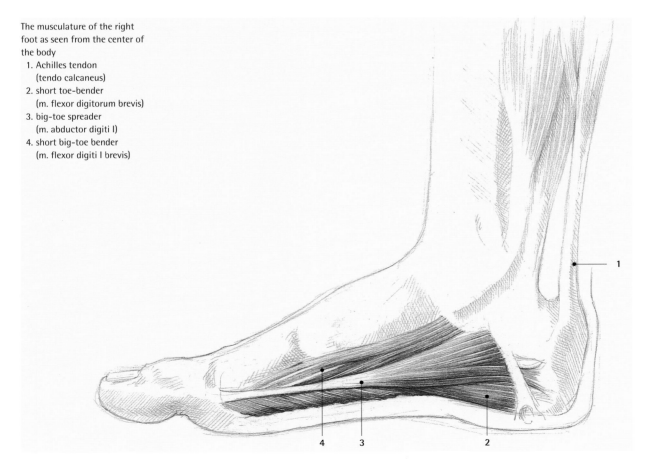

The musculature of the right
foot as seen from the center of
the body
1. Achilles tendon
   (tendo calcaneus)
2. short toe-bender
   (m. flexor digitorum brevis)
3. big-toe spreader
   (m. abductor digiti I)
4. short big-toe bender
   (m. flexor digiti I brevis)

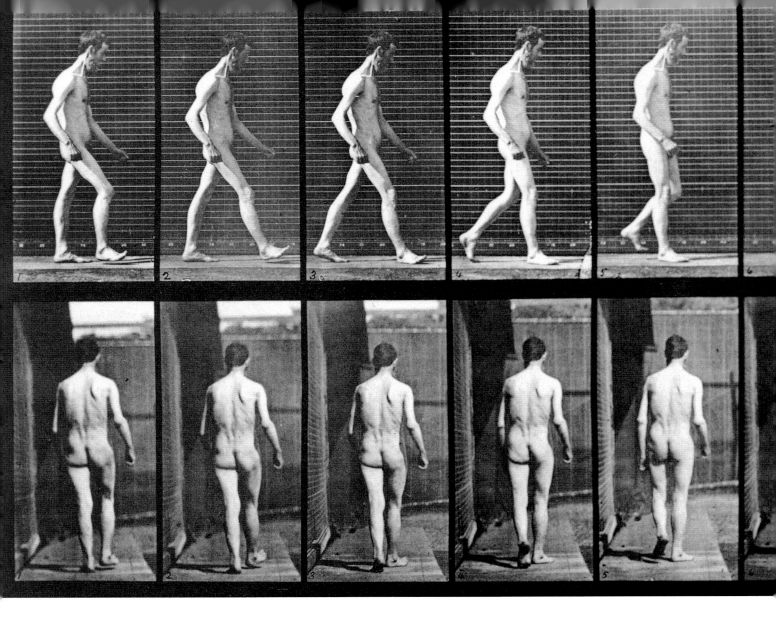

Phases of Walking

When we walk we place the soles of our feet on the ground alternately, at the same time either shifting or supporting the center of gravity of the body weight. With each step the body moves in the vertical plane, that is it rises and falls. But at the same time it also describes oblique and horizontal movements when the center of gravity of the body shifts from the side of the supporting leg to that of the other so that the body can maintain its equilibrium. When we walk we first raise the heel of the right foot, pressing the sole and the toes hard against the ground at the level of the metatarsals. Assisted by the toes, this foot then lifts off the ground. It is still in the air when the left foot begins to execute the same series of movements. The right foot returns to the ground, the entire body weight initially resting on its heel. In normal walking the foot is subjected to great pressure differentials: either it bears the whole body weight, or it floats "weightless" in the air.

Running is actually accelerated walking, with the difference that there is a time when neither foot is in

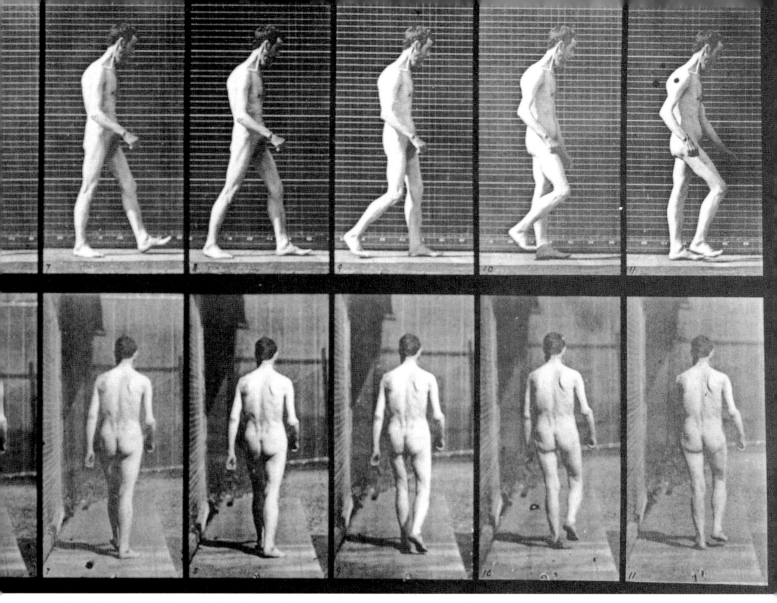

In 1901 Eadweard Muybridge produced 196 photographic plates with over 4,700 images of the human body in motion. He used one camera for each movement phase, that is eleven cameras for the phases shown here. He shot each image at 1/6000th of a second on a 10 x 13 cm glass plate.
From: Eadweard Muybridge, *The Human Figure in Motion*, Dover Publications, 1955, New York.

contact with the ground. The bones and musculature of the feet, as well as their networks of veins and nerves, constantly adapt to the strains imposed by the individual movement phases of walking, running, and jumping.

At the end of the nineteenth century the English photographer Eadweard Muybridge (1830–1904) achieved great fame in the United States. He invented a special method of capturing the separate phases of movement. Together with the painter Meissonier (who afterwards actually corrected the positions of horses' legs in two of his paintings) and the physiologist Marey he conceived a unique publication. He eventually published a lexicon containing some 100,000 negatives capturing the movement phases of the human body. Following this idea, shoemakers today often make video recordings of their clients walking in bare feet, in order to gather information that is important for the design of their new shoes. The increasing use of computers in conjunction with video technology should make shoe design a very precise operation.

The Arches

The sole of the foot does not make uniform contact with the ground. Instead the shape of the bones and the tendons and muscles connecting them mean that it rests on an arch curved in two planes: the lengthwise and the transverse. The outer lengthwise curve of the arch joins the heel bone to the little toe, the inner lengthwise curve joins the heel bone to the big toe, and finally the transverse curve joins the big and little toes to each other. When standing, the entire body weight rests on the three points where these curves intersect.

The arch changes shape when we walk. When it bears the body weight, for example, it falls by up to a quarter inch [5 mm], and the foot stretches. As soon as that load is no longer there, the foot regains its original shape. The arched structure acts as a shock absorber, reducing the impact on the head and spinal column of walking, and thus helping us to achieve a regular, uniform gait. The toes also have an important role to play in supporting the body. They too act as shock absorbers, and when the foot is lifted from the ground they make the motion flexible. The arch, which develops in childhood, is the result of correct or incorrect locomotion. Walking barefoot is the most suitable type of locomotion for the foot, because its musculature adapts in a self-regulating manner to any

ground unevenness. The muscles work ceaselessly, which stimulates the musculature and keeps it in good condition. All this ensures that the arch of the foot functions perfectly. Poor footwear impedes the natural movement of the foot, and problems with the feet lead sooner or later to more general postural disorders. It is therefore extremely important to have good footwear, and the only really satisfactory footwear in this respect is of the handmade variety. Mass-produced shoes can never be suitable, because every foot is different and adjustments need to be made to take account of this.

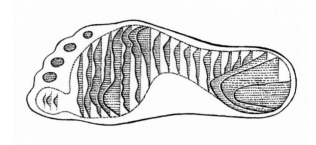

In a sound lengthwise arch the curve of the bones is ideal: the body weight rests on the heel, the inner and outer metatarsals, the outer rim of the sole, and the toes.

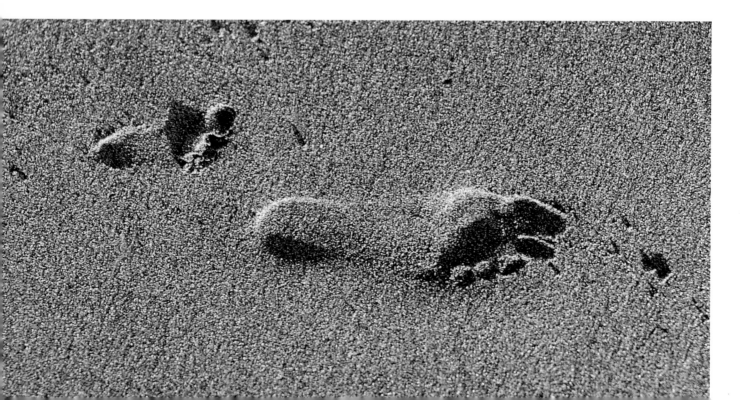

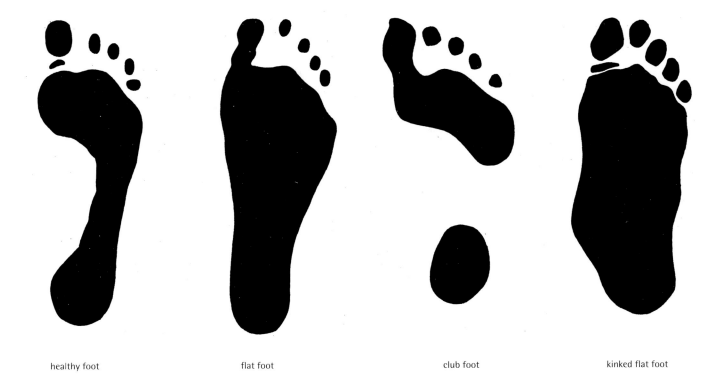

healthy foot   flat foot   club foot   kinked flat foot

Common Malformations

The "normal" foot is of average size (8–10 for men) and anatomically in proportion, that is taller people have larger feet. It has a pronounced arch, the musculature is firm, the skin surface smooth, and the volume of perspiration produced is always appropriate to the circumstances. Anybody who has feet as ideal as this may count himself fortunate, because most people don't.

If the proportions of the feet deviate from the average, this is sometimes due to anatomical factors and sometimes the result of functional causes. Men of above-average body weight generally have wide feet, and vice versa. Wide feet usually have high insteps, though these are also found in narrower feet. The proportions of the feet can change with time: active sports (running, fencing, football, tennis, and other vigorous sports) generally produce a firmer musculature, wider feet, and higher insteps.

The most common functional deviations are the various forms of fallen arches. These take the initial form of mere functional problems, such as excessive strain on the tendons and ligaments – but sooner or later they inevitably develop into flat feet. It is no longer the lower part of the heel bone that forms the support; this function is taken over by the forward part of it as it falls towards the sole. It is followed by the whole of the foot's arch structure. Flat feet lead to further malformations: to toes crossing over one another; to hammer toes, where the roots of the toes lift and buckle so that they are bent at an angle; or to deformations of the balls of the foot in which the angle between the big toe and its metatarsal bone is sharply reduced. All these changes are accompanied by hardening of the skin and corns.

Shoes that have been carefully made on the basis of accurate measurements admittedly can not cure conditions like these, but they can alleviate or even eliminate the pain that results from them. A master shoemaker can create shoes for an individual customer that will be comfortable on his feet and that will also make his whole body feel relaxed. Custom-made shoes are also esthetically pleasing, and so provide the best of both worlds – health and beauty!

Shoe Sizes

The footwear business has had a standard measure since the eighteenth century: the stitch measure. Parisian, Berlin, Viennese, and other stitches were used, which the craftsmen of the various regions had agreed to adopt as a designation of length. But until the mass production of shoes started at the end of the nineteenth century, the shoe size, designating the length of the shoe, was of no special importance.

The smaller shoe in this photograph is a French size 39. This is equivalent to English and American size 6 and metric size 26. The larger shoe is a French size 46, equivalent to an English 11, an American 11½, and a metric 30.

French Sizes

The use of the Parisian stitch just over a quarter inch [6.667 mm] long became widespread in Europe at the time of Napoleon (the beginning of the eighteenth century). But this measure was soon found to be insufficiently precise, and half-sizes were introduced in some countries. French size 40.5, for example, is equivalent to about 11 inches [27 cm].

English Sizes

The English system for measuring length was promulgated in 1324 at the behest of King Edward II. He decreed that three grains of barley were equal to one inch [2.54 cm] and 12 inches equal to one foot [30.48 cm]. So the standard measure of English shoe sizes is the length of a grain of barley, that is one-third of an inch [0.846 cm]. This unit also turned out to be too crude, and half-sizes also came to be used: 1 half-size = one-sixth of an inch [0.423 cm].

English shoe sizes for adults start at size 1, some eight-and-two-thirds inches [22 cm] long (equivalent to the French size 33). This length is increased by the requisite one-third of an inch for each size. The French size 42, for example, is roughly equal to metric size 28 and English size 8: 8 inches + (8 x $\frac{1}{3}$) = 10$\frac{1}{3}$ inches [22 cm + (8 x 0.846) = 28.77 cm]. The common shoe sizes for men are those between 5½ and 11, equivalent to French sizes 39 and 46 respectively.

It is becoming increasingly common for shoes available in England to be designated with both English and French sizes.

American Sizes (USA)

The American unit, 1 size, is the same as the English, but the difference lies in the starting-points: in the American system the scale begins one-twelfth of an inch [2.116 mm] lower, which means that each American size covers a rather lower range than its English equivalent. Yet another cause of Transatlantic confusion!

Metric Sizes

The metric system is just as suitable for measuring the length of a foot or a shoe as for anything else, and the metric scale does indeed exist. But for some reason it has never caught on as a designation of shoe sizes.

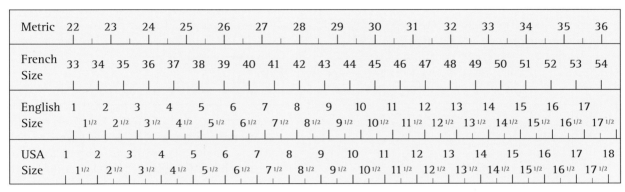

Metric	22	23	24	25	26	27	28	29	30	31	32	33	34	35	36

French Size	33 34 35 36 37 38 39 40 41 42 43 44 45 46 47 48 49 50 51 52 53 54

English Size	1	2	3	4	5	6	7	8	9	10	11	12	13	14	15	16	17
	1½	2½	3½	4½	5½	6½	7½	8½	9½	10½	11½	12½	13½	14½	15½	16½	17½

USA Size	1	2	3	4	5	6	7	8	9	10	11	12	13	14	15	16	17	18
	1½	2½	3½	4½	5½	6½	7½	8½	9½	10½	11½	12½	13½	14½	15½	16½	17½	

This table shows how the sizes in the various systems relate to each other.

Girth Measurements

The metric side of the tape measure is always used for girth measurements. To measure the metatarsals the shoemaker passes the tape measure beneath the sole of the foot between the outermost points of the inner and outer metatarsals at a slight angle to the transverse. About 2 inches [5–6 cm] nearer to the ankle he measures the girth of the instep. Next comes the girth of the heel, for which the tape measure is passed round the ankle bone and under the heel. If the shoemaker is making ankle boots or high boots, he also needs the girth of the ankle and for this he passes the tape measure round the leg below the ankle.

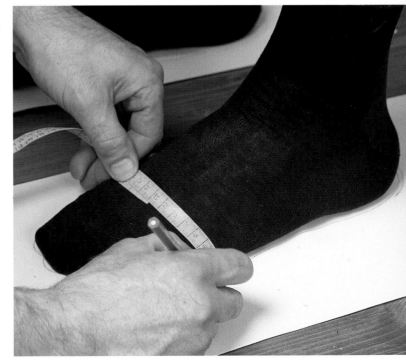

All girth measurements – here of the metatarsals – are taken with great care with the metric side of the tape measure.

Width Numbering

Differences of bone structure and musculature can mean that feet of the same length have very different girth (referred to here as width) measurements. It is therefore most expedient for both the shoemaker and the lastmaker to measure and tabulate these various widths. This is the background to the width-numbering system, in which 5 (E) denotes the narrowest foot, 6 (F) the average, 7 (G) wide, and 8 (H) very wide.

Since the ratios between the measurements of an average foot are constant, particular circumferential measurements are associated with particular lengths. Formulas exist enabling the shoe size (denoting length) and its associated width number to be used to calculate the width of the metatarsals, the instep, the heel, and the ankle. To obtain the width of the metatarsals, for example, the shoe size is added to the width number and the result halved: shoe size 42, average width 6, width of metatarsals 24. (This is one of the simpler formulas; in view of the complexity of the others we shall not consider them here.)

These formulas have been developed over many years, and are tried and tested. A customer can be confident that his shoemaker will use them accurately in order to assess the size of shoe needed for him.

Size *	width of metatarsals in cm									
	A (1)	B (2)	C (3)	D (4)	E (5)	F (6)	G (7)	H (8)	I (9)	
5	19,50	20,00	20,50	21,00	21,50	22,00	22,50	23,00	23,50	increase of
6	20,10	20,60	21,10	21,60	22,10	22,60	23,10	23,60	24,10	0.5 cm per
7	20,65	21,15	21,65	22,15	22,65	23,15	23,65	24,15	24,65	width
8	21,20	21,70	22,20	22,70	23,20	23,70	24,20	24,70	25,20	number
9	21,70	22,20	22,70	23,20	23,70	24,20	24,70	25,20	25,70	
10	22,25	22,75	23,25	23,75	24,25	24,75	25,25	25,75	26,25	
11	22,75	23,25	23,75	24,25	24,75	25,25	25,75	26,25	26,75	
12	23,30	23,80	24,30	24,80	25,30	25,80	26,30	26,80	27,30	

* The increase in width per size is not constant.

French size	size	metatarsal width	instep width	heel width	ankle width
			in cm		
39	26	22,5	23,3	32	22
40	26,7	23	24	32,7	22,5
41	27,3	23,5	24,5	33,3	23
42	28	24	25	34	23,5
43	28,7	24,5	25,5	34,7	24
44	29,3	25	26	35,3	24,5
45	30	25,5	26,5	36	25

With a tape measure and this table anybody with average-size feet and width number 6 (E) can determine his exact shoe size. If the various measurements agree exactly or deviate by no more than an eighth of an inch [0.2–0.3 cm], he will have no difficulty in finding perfectly comfortable ready-made shoes. Anybody finding more significant discrepancies is recommended to have his shoes custom made; this is the only way to obtain a pair that will fit him properly.

Foot ID

To the documents serving as proof of identity – our fingerprints, for example, or our dental records – we could well add our foot imprint and measurements held by our shoemaker, for the characteristic data of our feet are just as individual, and just as much of a giveaway, as the whorls and loops on the skin of our fingertips.

As the measurements are taken, the dimension sheet for the left and right feet fills up with more and more data. After the draft has been calculated, the girth measurements are entered and the critical points and features that deviate from the norm are marked; and the shoemaker also summarizes all the information that he has gathered during his discussion with his customer, when palpating his feet, observing his gait, and examining his old shoes. If the customer wears inserts to support his arches, the shoemaker measures their thickness, length, and height and enters these details on the dimension sheets too, for in the light of this information he will certainly have to make the shoes wider and give them higher sides. It is also helpful for the shoemaker to elicit information about any internal complaints the customer may have, like circulatory problems, rheumatic complaints, or diabetes. In these cases lighter, lace-up shoes are advisable in order to avoid injurious consequences such as diabetic foot or inflammatory bruises.

In the light of all these details the type, leather, and color of the shoes are now selected – and also entered in the dimension record – which, together with the foot imprint, the draft drawings, and the marked-up last, now form the basis on which the custom-made last will be produced. The dimensions of the feet do not change over the years, except in special circumstances like a drastic increase in weight, so the custom-made last can be used for an extended period without new measurements being taken. However, it is thought advisable to check the measurements of the last every two or three years, just in case any unusual change in dimensions has occurred. There is always a first time for everything, and both shoemaker and customer need to feel confident that the data collected is still relevant and suitable for use in making the shoes.

A

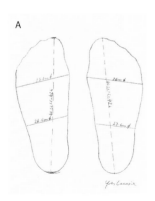

B

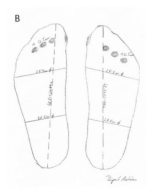

C

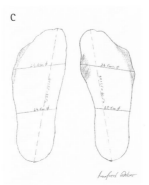

The lines, numberings, and shadings of the outline drawings show how individual the feet are. In A, for example, the girths are above the average, and the right foot is bigger than the left. In B the black circles mark hammer toes, while in C the right foot is a 40.5, the left a 41.5. The black shading marks heavy swelling of the metatarsals.

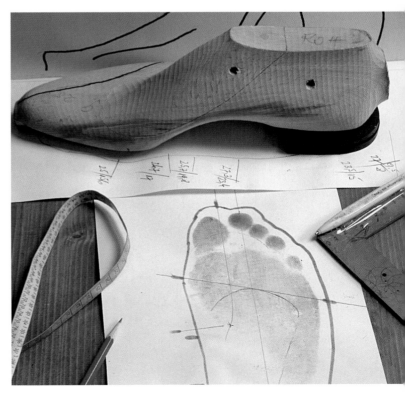

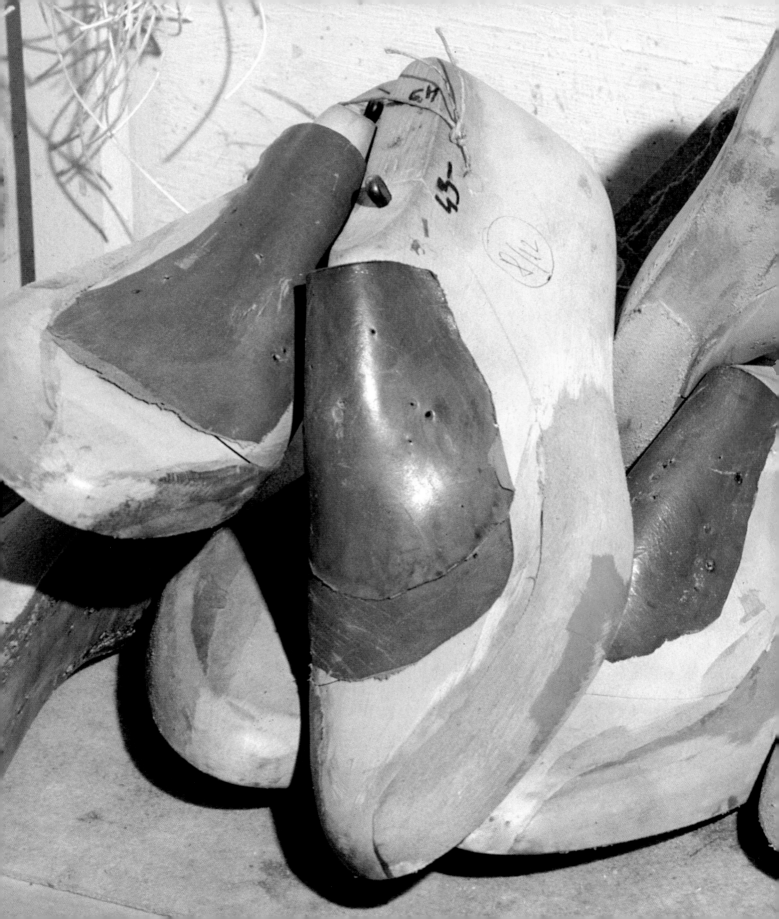

Lasts

Why do we Need Lasts?

The last is an abstract copy of the human foot in wood. One of its functions is to take the place of the foot in the production phases as a working surface on which flat leather components can be given plastic form.

The second important function is that the last corresponds to the favored fashion trend and to esthetic requirements, in that its shape is as close to perfection as the type of shoes chosen. In this respect no extreme fashion shifts have been discernible in the field of gentlemen's footwear in the last 100 years. There are a few basic models that differ primarily in the shape of the toe caps, the pattern of the uppers, and the decoration. Types of last have developed accordingly, most of them designated by the same name as the shoes made on them – hence the Budapest last, for example, which has characteristic high toe caps.

The last, which determines both the internal dimensions and the external shape of the shoe, is prepared in accordance with the measurements taken – and always in pairs. In the last chapter we saw that the right foot is not a mirror image of the left: the two feet may differ marginally, or sometimes even substantially, in both shape and size. A good lastmaker reads off the tiniest deviations from the dimension sheets and incorporates them in the lasts.

There are hardly any lastmakers left in the world who insist on working only with their hands, only occasionally resorting to machine processing to make their laborious work less onerous. In this chapter we shall follow the painstaking processes by which lasts are produced, in a unique workshop where traditional tools are still used, meticulously creating the flawless lasts without which no perfect pair of custom-made shoes could ever come into being. The making of the last is as important as any other process involved in the creation of shoes, and needs to be carried out with great care.

The custom-made last is an abstract form in wood, created on the basis of the data gathered during the measurement-taking process. On the one hand it takes the place of the customer's foot while the shoe is being constructed, and on the other it already has the characteristics of the selected type of shoe.

"The Cobbler Should Stick to his Last!"

The most important tool in the shoemaker's craft, and at the same time its symbol, is the last. Its origins lie almost as far back in the mists of time as those of the craft itself. The first concrete evidence of the use of the last in shoemaking can be found in Greek and Roman antiquity. Plato (427–347 BC), the Greek philosopher, relates in his "Symposion" how Zeus, when he created man, assembled him from two components, sewing him together at the navel. He smoothed out the wrinkles and fitted the torso, "using the tool with which the shoemaker smoothes out creases in the leather."

The Roman writer Pliny the Elder (23–79 AD) also relates an amusing anecdote, about the dispute between the artist Apelles and a shoemaker. Apelles, a famous painter of Greek antiquity (he worked between 340 and 300 BC – unhappily none of his works has survived), used to set up his latest work in the porch of his house, then hide behind a panel to hear what the common people thought of it; he thought they were more conscientious judges than he was. On one such occasion a "sutor" (shoemaker) noticed that an eyelet was missing on the inner side of a shoe. With a smile the painter corrected this mistake. When the shoemaker, encouraged by this, started to criticize other aspects of the leg of the figure, Apelles snarled at him: "*Ne supra crepidam sutor iudicet!*" (The shoemaker should look no higher than the sandal!) This was the origin of today's saying: "The cobbler should stick to his last!"

Greek shoemakers used the last to fit straps to their sandals, Roman shoemakers used it to sew together shoes that they had already assembled.

They distinguished by shoe type and size between various types of last for sandals and closed shoes. They were also familiar with the asymmetric last, that is, one distinguishing between the right and left feet. They made separate lasts for each foot, even making collapsible lasts for bootmaking.

This ancient art was passed down through the generations, and slowly developed into the form that we know today. But there were some periods in history when the skill of lastmaking seemed to be threatened with being forgotten.

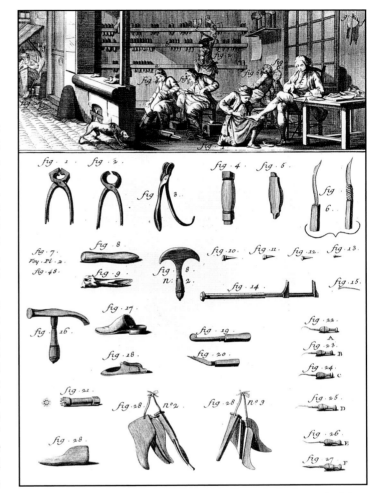

The last is the shoemaker's most important tool. This is a copperplate illustration by Robert Benard for the *Encyclopédie ou Dictionnaire raisonné des Sciences, des Arts et des Métiers* (1751–1781) by D. Diderot and J.B. D'Alembert.

There are two lasts in the tympanum of the gravestone of C. Julius Helius (first half of the second century AD); the left-hand one has a thong sandal on it in the process of construction (Capitoline Museum, Rome).

The Symmetric Last and the Asymmetric Last

As the Middle Ages approached, knowledge of lastmaking – as of so much else – was entirely lost. In all probability footwear was made without the use of any tools in northern Europe during this period, shoemakers simply sewing pieces of leather together in something approximating to the right shape. Only in the sixteenth century are there numerous engravings, drawings, and paintings which once more provide evidence of the use of tools, of lasts in particular. As in antiquity, shoemakers held stocks of standard lasts – individual lasts, as they are today, being produced only for selected customers or by special request. Initially all that was used was a thick wooden plate in the shape of the sole, with wooden attachments to make it easier to remove when the shoe was finished (see drawing). It must have been necessary to use a divided, asymmetric last for the long, pointed shoes called poulaines, which had small openings for the feet, but towards the end of the Middle Ages – at the time of the typically medieval peasant shoe, with its regular, wide shape and large opening (see pages 56–57) – shoemakers were still working with undivided, symmetric lasts. They took measurements from one foot for both lasts, which understandably made the process of breaking in the shoes acutely unpleasant for the wearer. No wonder noblemen would often break in new pairs of shoes by making their valets wear them for six months.

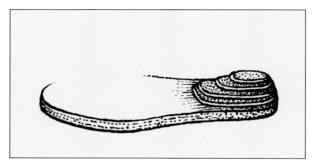

Last with wooden attachments.

The asymmetric last was "rediscovered" at the beginning of the nineteenth century. The starting point for this was the interest in primeval man that became widespread during the Enlightenment (beginning at the end of the seventeenth century and extending into the nineteenth) under the slogan "Back to Nature." It was reason – according to such philosophers as Locke, Rousseau, Hume, and Pestalozzi – that should determine human thought and action. As part of this trend, society developed a more natural and wholesome consciousness of the body that was reflected in fashion. Initial efforts made in this direction related to soldiers' footwear: it was felt that in view of the demands made on it, it should be made more comfortable. Shoemakers began to base their work on the natural foot and to study its anatomy – which has remained an important part of the shoemaker's training to this day, particularly since the definitive adoption of the asymmetric last at the beginning of the twentieth century.

The demand for well-fitting shoes has been constantly rising since the nineteenth century. The development of mass production led to a new division of labor and the more pronounced separation of the various trades involved. Today, as a result of the process of industrialization that engulfed shoemaking during the second half of the nineteenth century, making lasts by hand is a rare and particular skill.

These original lasts (in the Württemberg Regional Museum, Stuttgart) date from the fifth or sixth centuries AD. They were found in graves near Oberflacht, Germany.

This Gothic-style leather, side-laced poulaine from around 1420 contains an original asymmetric, divided last (Bally Footwear Museum, Schönenwerd).

The traditionally prepared lasts of Emperor Franz Joseph I of Austria (1848–1916) are carefully preserved by the Scheer shoemaking workshop in Vienna.

The awareness of the need for different lasts for the right and left feet was lost during the Middle Ages, when shoemakers always worked with a single symmetric last. This is a quite recent example from the workshop of Ferenc Felbert in Köszeg, Hungary, 1890–1920.

The Raw Material of the Last

The last can only carry out its function perfectly, that is high-quality shoes can only be produced on it, if it is made from the very best timber. Certain parts of the shoe – like the molds of the toe caps or heel cups, for example – are actually impossible to process properly except on a last made from timber that is hard, yet has the requisite degree of resilience. The only possible raw material for this last is wood that is resistant to both fluctuating humidity and temperature differences and can stand up to heavy pressure, hammer blows, and having nails driven into it. Woods satisfying these conditions include maple, beech, oak, elm, and walnut, but it is only the European beech and the hornbeam that fill the bill completely and are therefore the most economical wood for lastmaking.

The lastmaker selects his wood while it is still in the ground. He knows that trees growing in a rocky area always produce harder wood than trees growing in meadows or near water. He observes the development of the trees over a period of many years and notes any growth defects, for wood from trees that fail to grow straight, or that have been attacked by woodworm or fungus, should not be used. The trunks of the trees selected should be at least 12–16 inches [30–40 cm] thick. The hornbeam grows very slowly, and it will be some 80–100 years old before its trunk is thick enough to enable high-quality lasts of the requisite size to be produced from it. The chosen tree is felled when its fluid circulation is at its slowest, which in Europe is between November and February. The wood from trees felled at this time of the year dries faster and is harder.

This attention to detail is vital in the lastmaker's art, and it requires many years' experience for the skill to reach the necessary level.

The beech (*Fagus sylvatica*): Europe's most important broad-leaf tree is indigenous to mountainous regions up to a height of 2600 feet [800 m]. There are several species, among them the European beech, the white beech, the copper beech, the stone beech, the hanging beech, the hop beech, and the weeping beech. Its pale-yellow or reddish wood is slow drying and easy to work, polish, and heat treat.

The hornbeam (*Carpinus betulus*), which is found in hilly and mountainous areas, is tolerant of shade and less sensitive to extreme climatic conditions. Its bark is thin, smooth, and pale gray, and it has striking broad, light-colored vertical stripes. Its sapwood and heartwood are white, but they turn yellowish when exposed to the air. The hornbeam trunk is tall, virtually cylindrical, and hence very economical to process.

The lastmaker orders his selected timber two or even three years before using it. The tree is felled in winter, sawn up into lengths of 6½ feet [2 m], stacked, and stored for a number of months in the open. While the timber rests, the slow drying process begins, and its moisture content falls from 50–60% to 25–30%.

Raw timber is extraordinarily sensitive, its volume changing rapidly as a result of fluctuations in air temperature or humidity. This is why the timing and duration of the natural drying process must be so carefully considered. Excessive heat or strong sunlight can dry the wood out too much, and it is liable to shatter like glass at the lightest of blows.

Cutting It Up

In the workshop a block of wood some 12–13 inches [30–32 cm] long is cut up into four or six blocks, depending on the age and diameter of the tree, each of which becomes a last. The lengthwise axis of the lasts must lie along the grain of the wood.

Economy is an important factor when the block is cut up: thicker trees are used to make larger lasts and vice versa. Once cut up, the pieces of wood are carefully examined and sorted. Only wood in first-class condition can stand up to the treatment it will receive in shoe manufacture: hammering, nails, and moisture. The economic thickness of a length of trunk is generally 14–20 inches [35–50 cm]. The innermost part is the heart or pith, in young trees still soft and spongy, around which the annual rings subsequently form and from which the lasts will eventually be produced.

The lastmaker can in effect already see the completed last in his mind's eye while it is still concealed in the wood. He relies on his eye and on his many years of experience when he uses a jigsaw, or the more traditional guillotine, to form a segment of the block that subsequent processes will turn into the last.

A 6½-foot [2 m] section of tree trunk is sawn up into pieces about 13 inches [32 cm] long. There is no need to remove the bark, as it will fall off during subsequent processing.

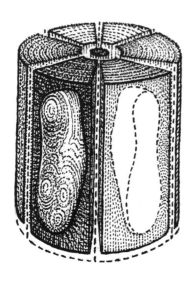

From four to six lasts can be produced from a length of trunk 14–20 inches [35–50 cm] in diameter, the economic thickness.

Heat-Treating and Drying

The rough-cut blocks of hornbeam or European beech are placed in a cylindrical chamber and heat-treated at a pressure of two to three atmospheres and a temperature of 250°F [120°C] to destroy unbonded fluids, acids, and fungi and render the wood insensitive to moisture and temperature differences. Some 7 ounces [200 g] of water is evaporated from an 18-ounce [500 g] block of wood. The fibers of the wood become denser and at the same time more resilient. When a nail is driven into a piece of wood that has been heat-treated, the fibers are forced apart; when the nail is removed, they return to their original positions.

After heat-treating, both ends of the blocks are coated with wax so that in subsequent drying the fluid in the wood will evaporate at the lateral surfaces and the ends will not crack. Now the period of natural drying begins; this lasts some two years. Although the moisture content of the wood falls to 16–18% over this period, it must be further reduced to 10–12% before it can undergo further processing. Forced drying in the drying chamber lasts about three weeks. The blocks of wood are exposed to an airflow initially at a temperature of 68°F [20°C], which is gradually raised to 85–100°F [30–40°C] and finally to 120°F [50°C]. The moisture content of the wood is checked continually.

Neither forced nor natural drying (storage in a shed) can be hurried. If the blocks of wood are put into the dryer too soon, for example, most of them will crack or become deformd, losing the very quality for which they were selected for lastmaking: their resilience. After many years of preparation the block of wood is ready for delivery to the lastmaker's workshop to be made into a last. In the following pages we shall find out some of the secrets of the lastmaker's art and how a good-quality last is made – the basis of a good-quality shoe.

For the period of natural drying and resting the wax-coated blocks of wood are stacked in a covered shed in such a way that each of them is exposed on all sides to an adequate airflow with an average moisture content of 16–18%. During the slow drying period the moisture content of the wood will also fall to this level, making it suitable for converting into lasts.

The Lastmaker

The Berta lastmaking workshop founded in Pápa, Hungary, in 1870 is the only one of its kind in the country, supplying top-class shoemaking workshops in England, Austria, Germany, the Netherlands, and Italy with lasts and shoe trees. Kálmán Berta, now 78, is one of the few true masters of his subject in Europe: "My father was a lastmaker, and his father before him. Most of our tools have been handed down from generation to generation, just like our love of the craft. My grandfather Márton traveled to Germany in 1867 to learn the art of lastmaking there. He visited several places before reaching the town of Pirmasens, the last stage of his journey, where he found a lastmaker willing to initiate him into the secrets of manual lastmaking. He worked there for more than two years. In the nineteenth century Pirmasens was one of the strongholds of the shoemaker's craft. Over a well in its castle square there was a statue of a shoemaker by the name of Joss, holding a last in one hand and a shoemaker's hammer in the other.

"My grandfather used to carve symmetric lasts based on a paper form. Once he had passed the guild examination by producing a last that met with the approval of its members, he returned to Hungary, where

he laid the foundation stone for his workshop 125 years ago. He built a cable-driven machine that made the heavy carving work a bit easier, and carried on using it until 1911 – when he went to Vienna and bought a state-of-the-art duplicator and a planing machine.

"In the 1930s, I remember, members of the family used to go round selling the lasts we made in our little workshop. Every week or two there used to be a market in the Komitat, the largest Hungarian administrative unit, where you could get shoes, lasts, clothing, and other everyday requirements. On those days we used to load our lasts onto a horse-drawn wagon before dawn, take them to market, and offer them to the shoemakers.

"I learned the tricks of the trade from my father and grandfather in my childhood. A good lastmaker 'senses' the wood with his fingertips and palms, he can tell the lie of the fibers inside it, and knows where and how he must use the saw and the knife to remove only the excess wood. A good lastmaker knows instinctively how to make a good last from the basic block of wood. His skill is the 'soul' of the last.

"The shoemaker and the lastmaker speak the same language, because each of them has an intimate knowledge of the other's work. The shoemaker knows that fine, comfortable shoes can only be made on a well-formed last, and the lastmaker must have a mental picture of the shoe that is going to be made on the last. Even after 60 years my heart beats faster every time I approach the guillotine to create a new last."

Kálmán Berta can be seen here concentrating on producing yet another fine last, one of the many that he has produced over the decades. It is to be hoped that he has been able to pass on his admirable skills to new generations of lastmakers. A family tradition such as that of the Bertas must not be allowed to die out – it would be a tragedy if it did.

Shoemaker Joss is seen as one of the founding fathers of the shoemaking industry in Pirmasens. His statue, with the last – the symbol of his craft – in his left hand and a shoemaker's hammer in his right, stands in the town's pedestrian precinct and is its emblem.

Preparing the Custom-made Last by Hand

Many lastmakers' workshops still contain tools that have been in use for over a hundred years. Two of them from Kálmán Berta's workshop would not be out of place in a museum. One of these is a long-bladed guillotine used for the initial shaping of the last block: it's hooked onto one end of the workbench and can be moved freely, in both vertical and horizontal directions.

Once the block has been shaped with the guillotine, the lining sole, shaped with the assistance of the draft, is drawn on one side of it. The lastmaker then saws off its wax-coated ends and begins to shape it with the axe.

The block is laid on the workbench and repeatedly turned in the direction from which it can be most easily reached with the guillotine blade. The lastmaker applies the guillotine at a suitable angle and presses down on its handle to remove shavings of the desired thickness from the appropriate points. Even at this early stage he is guided by the data in the customer's measurement record regarding the length, girth, and type of the shoes required.

The finer bulges and hollows are produced with the wood-carving knife and the rasp, which is then used to refine them; this process also removes the marks left by tools used earlier, as well as any surface unevennesses. After making his final measurements the lastmaker will use sandpaper – first coarse, then increasingly fine – to give the last its ultimate form and a completely smooth surface.

These are the skills involved in making a last by hand, but there is also a long tradition of the use of machinery – to a limited degree – in making a last. Most lastmakers today will use a duplicator.

Preshaping

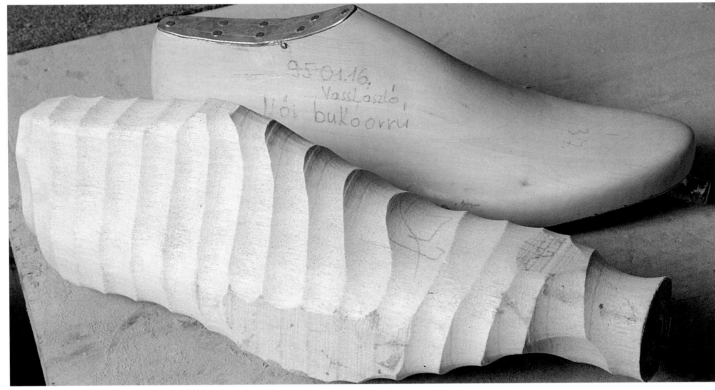

The lastmaker uses the duplicator to make the block (front) into a rough copy of a form (back).

Because shaping the last by hand is extraordinarily laborious and time-consuming, the so-called duplicator is now used throughout the world. The American Thomas Blanchard patented this type of lathe – which can produce irregular shapes in wood, such as rifle butts and, indeed, lasts – in Massachusetts, USA, in 1819. His invention was the basis of machines with which lasts – first symmetric, later asymmetric – were produced. In the 1920s the predecessor of the duplicators used today came on the market; it was capable of producing left and right lasts at the same time. Present-day machines take only five or six minutes to produce a pair of lasts.

If, for example, the figures on the measurement sheet for the length of the customer's feet and the girth of his metatarsals indicate that he needs a size 8½, medium width, but that both insteps are above average height, a form of size 9, width 7 is selected. If his feet are of different lengths, for example the left is an 8 and the right an 8½, then the formes selected are of sizes 8½ and 9 respectively. In the first case the right and left lasts are copied simultaneously from the form mounted in the duplicator, while in the second a size 8½ left rough last and a size 9 right rough last are made separately.

The use of the duplicator may have been frowned on when it was first introduced, but today it is accepted as necessary to the lastmaker's trade. It certainly does not mean that he requires any less skill to produce the lasts – only that he can save time by using this valuable machine.

Rough Copying   # Fine Copying

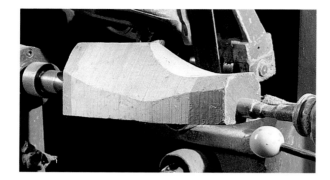

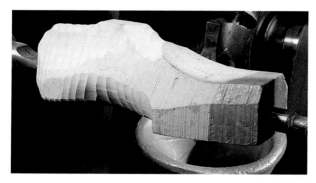

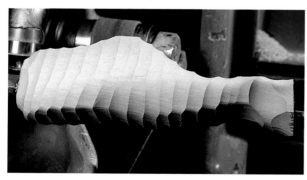

Two heat-treated and wax-coated blocks of wood are mounted in the duplicator and rough lasts for both feet are simultaneously copied from the form. A sensing system automatically follows the shape of the form and guides the sharp-edged cutter heads. The two wooden blocks rotate in opposite directions beneath the cutter heads, enabling the right and left lasts to be shaped simultaneously. Here the machine executes the rough-copying process, the initial stage in the shaping of the duplicate last.

When the lastmaker changes the machine setting to fine, the shaping process is continued with meticulous accuracy. The cutting heads are replaced by abrasive wheels, which first eradicate the edges of the grooves left by the cutting heads and then, working from the heel to the tip and back again, remove thin layers of wood until the last is the same shape and size as the form. Modern duplicators are capable of producing copies accurate to minute fractions of an inch, so making the lastmaker's task that much easier.

Final Adjustments

The lastmaker saws off the ends by which the lasts were mounted in the duplicator. He then drills a horizontal hole (picture top left) through the instep to make the last easier to remove from the completed shoe. The next process has a similar purpose: since the last cannot be removed in one piece, a gently curving wedge is sawn out of it (picture top right). While the shoe is being made this wedge must not protrude, so the lastmaker drills a vertical hole through both pieces, inserts a locating stud in it, and bolts them together (picture above).

The shoemakers of ancient Rome used divided lasts to make closed shoes so that they would be easy to remove once the shoes were finished. This is an example dating from about the second century AD from Rottweil, Germany (in the Württemberg Regional Museum in Stuttgart).

Custom-made Lasts

The Removal Method

Two typical methods are generally used to shape rough lasts into custom-made lasts, a process known as 'fitting up'. In the first method the last is given its individual shape by taking material away, in the second by adding it. The completed rough lasts – which are always slightly larger than required – finally reach the shoemaker's workshop. If the foot is narrower or the instep lower than the average, the shoemaker – guided by the measurement sheet – uses his rasp and various grades of sandpaper to give the last its ultimate form; in other words he takes material away.

The completed last is then roughened up with fine sandpaper so that the various types of leather will not slide this way and that on its surface when the shoe is being made.

The Addition Method

This lastmaking method recalls the most venerable traditions. Here, too, corrections are made in line with the measurement sheets, taking account of critical points. The characteristic places where the lastmaker most often has to make corrections are the outer rim of the sole, the metatarsals, the big toe, the instep, and the heel. It is extremely unusual for the foot to be smaller than the average at these places. It is far more common for the foot to be wider – for example, the instep and the big toe higher or the heel thicker. In the addition method the last is built up into the correct shape by sticking on various pieces of leather of the required thickness. If the deviation is very large, several layers of leather can be placed on top of one another.

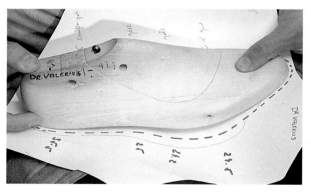

The edges of the pieces of leather are tapered.

In the removal method the lastmaker uses rasps – first coarse, then fine – to remove unwanted wood from the last.

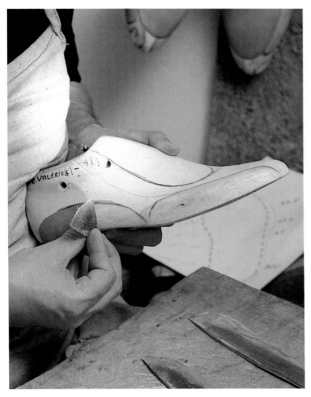

Additions are stuck on at the appropriate points.

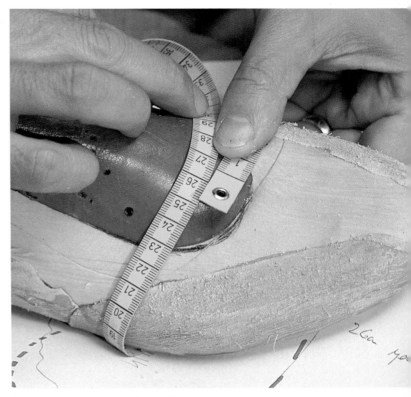

The measurements are checked frequently.

Corrected Custom-made Lasts

It is easy for the shoemaker to construct a pair of shoes on lasts produced by the addition method, that is by having pieces of leather stuck on. But the leather may get misshapen during the process, or even fall off. So if the customer wants several pairs of shoes to be made for him on the same set of lasts, it is safer to use the built-up lasts as formes for making final custom-made lasts.

The left and right lasts, corrected with leather attachments, are returned to the lastmaker's workshop, where they are used as formes for making new custom-made lasts. A prefabricated but slightly larger last is processed with the abrasive wheels. Within a few minutes the fine-copying process produces the custom-made last appropriate to the type of shoe.

The last is now ready to be used to make shoes. The shoemaker will examine the new last carefully to make sure it fulfils his requirements.

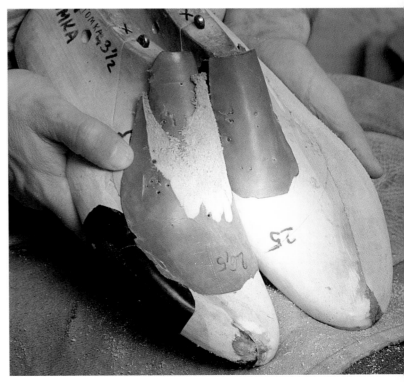

The lasts with leather attachments serve as formes for the final lasts, which embody all the features of the customer's feet.

Characteristic Custom-made Lasts

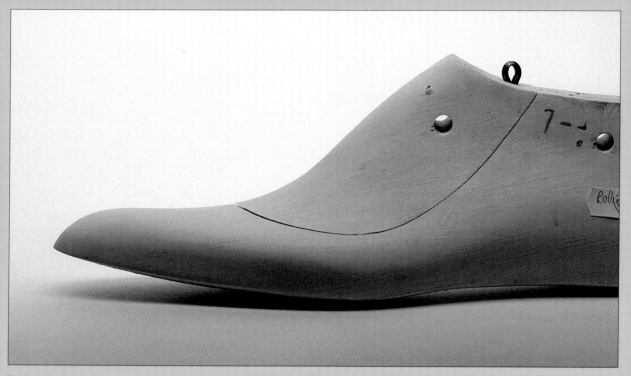

The German type features a high instep.

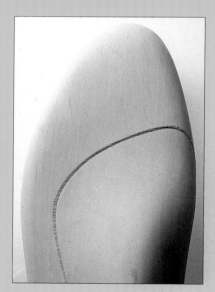

The German type also has an oval toe cap.

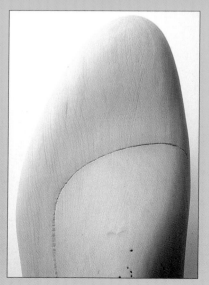

The banana-shaped Viennese type has a lowered transverse arch.

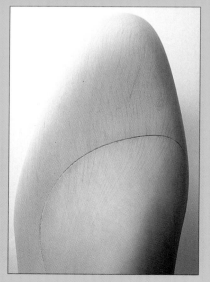

The open Italian type has a noticeably flat toe cap compared to other types.

The Austrian type has a characteristic instep.

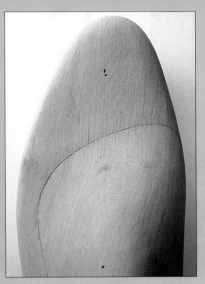

The Budapest type has a high toe cap.

The English type has a slightly angular toe cap.

Putting the Last to the Test

It is the responsibility of the shoemaker to obtain the right type of last for his client. Although any model of shoe can be made on any type of last, it is traditional for Derbys to be made on a German or Budapest last and Oxfords on an English last. The custom-made last has to have all the characteristic features of the last type, the individual foot, and the selected model of shoe.

Perfect shoes can only be made on perfect lasts, which is why most workshops insist on preparing a pair of trial shoes – an expensive additional task – in order to reduce the risk of disappointing the customer with an ill-fitting pair of shoes, and of wasting both expensive, top-quality leather and the time spent on making them. The shoemaker uses medium-quality leather for the trial shoes,

and he carries out all the processes described in the following chapters in simplified form. If the shoes prove comfortable, then the lastmaker has done a good job. If they are a poor fit at certain points, adjustments can be made to the last: the shoemaker marks the points on the last that must be built up or reduced. After this the trial shoes have served their purpose, and no further use is made of them.

This is all part of an involved process that will ultimately make sure that the customer is satisfied with his shoes.

The After-life of the Last

A perfect custom-made last can be used for many, many years. It is marked with the customer's name and stored in a room at a suitable air temperature and humidity so that the wood will retain its shape and resilience. The shoemaker can use it to make new, comfortable shoes whenever the customer requires.

After a period of two or three years, however, it is advisable to check the measurements of the last. The dimensions of the feet can change for the most diverse reasons, for example if the customer gains or loses weight, engages in high-intensity sport, suffers various illnesses, or develops malformations of the feet as time passes. In this event his measurements must be taken again and the last adjusted. If there have been no significant changes, the shoemaker can continue to use the same last.

New lasts are required in any case if the customer decides on a new model of shoe. Fashions change, and a customer's requirements change with them, although a classic shoe can never date.

The English company Lobb keeps 16,000 lasts in its
store rooms. Among them are wooden replicas of such
prominent feet as those of Fred Astaire, Enrico Caruso,
Fyodor Chaliapin, Andrew Carnegie, Bernard
Oppenheimer, Joseph Pulitzer, and others who have
been customers over the years.

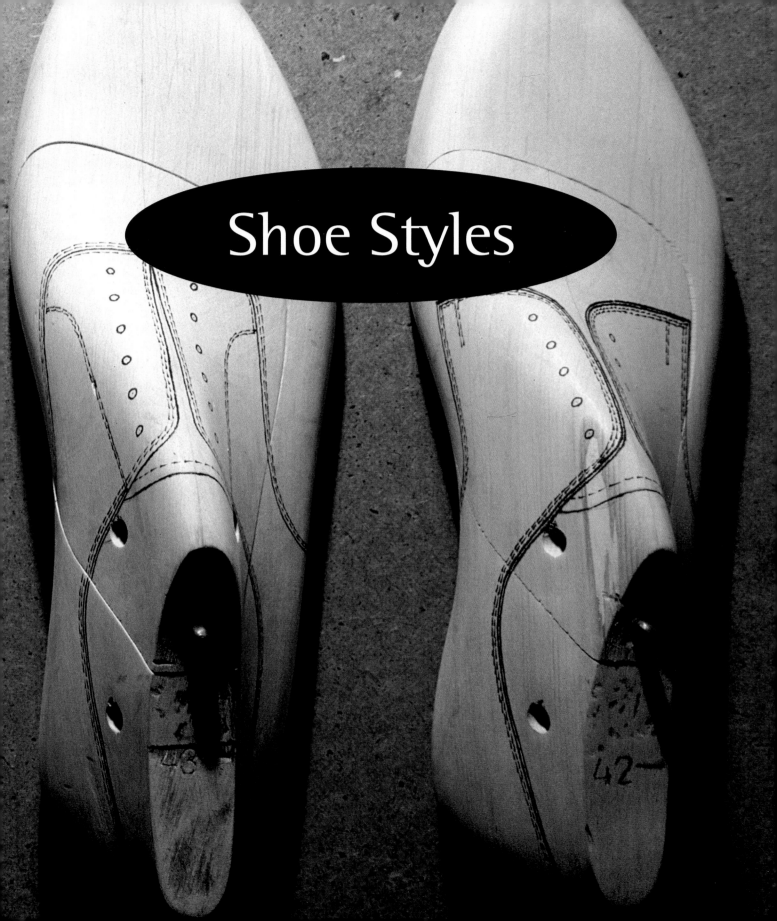

Shoe Styles

"Shoes Makyth Man"

Humans developed the need to protect their feet against adverse weather conditions early on in their history. This is proved by wall paintings in Spain dating from the period between 15,000 and 12,000 BC. The first basic forms of the shoe were simple foot coverings made of animal skin as well as primitive sandals of bast, palm leaves, and, later, wood.

The need for foot protection soon gave rise to a desire for shoes that would demonstrate individuality and social status: the more important the wearer, the more magnificent and individualistic his shoes would be. Membership of a social group was often signaled by a particular type of shoe (of a set style and with set decoration). Indeed, this social function may be regarded as the origin of the first fashions in shoes.

In Ancient Egypt senior priests and members of the ruling class were entitled to wear sandals made of silver or decorated with jewels. An important office at the court of the pharaoh was associated with this privilege. As early as the 1st Dynasty (2850-2660 BC) sandal-bearers worked at the holy places, which could only be entered barefoot. They watched over the precious sandals of the dignitaries or held them on a cushion behind the owner's back during certain rituals. This job continued in existence into the modern era.

Julius Caesar chose golden boots for official ceremonies, while Nero preferred silver sandals. Charlemagne wore shoes richly set with precious stones on festive occasions, and his son Louis I, known as Louis the Pious, felt golden boots to be worthy of his position. Until the nineteenth century elaborately decorated shoes were reserved for the richest members of society and there were, of course, strict rules governing what could be worn by someone of a particular rank. The middle classes (the lower aristocracy and prosperous merchants) possessed shoes that were considerably less elaborate, while poor people wore clogs or simple shoes tied at the ankle with a leather strap. Some people even went barefoot.

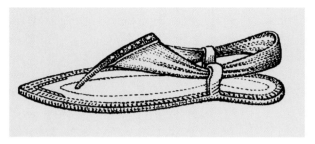

This palm-leaf sandal (Thebes, Upper Egypt, 1400-1250 BC) fulfilled the basic demands made on shoes: a sole held onto the foot with straps provided protection when walking on sand or stones.

This silver sandal found in an Egyptian grave of the Byzantine period is in many ways similar to the palm-leaf sandal. The precious materials and the rich decoration of an otherwise simple design show that shoes were a symbol of affluence and social status as early as the sixth century (Bally Schuhmuseum, Schönenwerd).

The red material and the Greek cross stitched in gold thread indicate that this slipper belonged to a man of the Church. The inscription on the insole, "Portatur a sss Patre Pius VI. to," identifies it as the property of Pope Pius VI (1775-1779) (Bayrisches Nationalmuseum, Munich).

The shoes of Napoleon I (1769-1821), who wore these simple pumps with low heels at his coronation in 1804. Tradition has it that Napoleon showed his superiority to the pope by taking the crown from the pope's hands and placing it on his own head, so crowning himself. Further proof of his superiority can be seen in the fact that his shoes were much more elaborately decorated than those of the head of the Church (formerly located at the Rüstkammer der Sächsischen Landes-bibliothek, Dresden, which was destroyed during the war).

Workers also tried to protect their feet as best they could. They made shoes out of hard, robust materials without decoration, as shown in closely observed, realistic detail in Gustave Courbet's painting *The Stone Crushers* (1849). (Former holding of the Gemäldegalerie Dresden, destroyed during the war).

Footwear Fashions

From the beginning, fashions in men's footwear were dominated by the boot, which was regarded as a particularly masculine kind of footwear. However, shoes also appeared in many forms, which varied with the spirit of the times. Like fashions in ladies' shoes, men's footwear was subject to often unpredictable and dramatic changes.

The first wave of fashion swept over Europe in the twelfth and thirteenth centuries. The crusaders introduced a modern adaptation of the pointed shoes worn by the Assyrians and, later, the Etruscans. This was the poulaine, an extremely long version of the pointed shoe that had been worn since late antiquity (fifth/sixth century AD). It was worn with a patten, which was a wooden overshoe that provided support and helped to keep the wearer's feet dry when he walked in the street. No other shoe has ever caused such a stir! With time the "pike" of the poulaine, which was reserved mainly for courtiers and the richer merchants, grew to ridiculous lengths as those who wore them sought to use them as markers of social status. Of course, the excesses of the extended poulaine also had evident phallic connotations. In the end, a papal edict was issued with the aim of reducing the length of pointed shoes to within the bounds of reason. The French king Philip IV, known as Philip the Fair, proclaimed that dukes could wear pointed shoes that were two-and-a-half times as long as their feet, while the shoes of the higher nobility could be no more than twice, and those of knights only one-and-a-half times, the length of their feet.

The poulaine conveys an unmistakable sexual message in this copperplate engraving by Israhel von Meckenems dating from the fifteenth century (Staatliche Graphische Sammlung, Munich).

In 1436 King Edward IV of England set out restrictions on shoe length in law: "No man beneath the rank of a lord may use or wear shoes or boots of any kind with a point longer than 2 inches [5 cm]; otherwise he must pay the crown a fine of three shillings and four pence for each infringement."

Around 1500, with the Renaissance and the rise of the urban bourgeoisie, a very simple, wide shoe came into fashion, though, unlike the poulaine, this was the basic shoe worn by all sectors of society. Logically enough, this countermovement to the courtly, pointed shoe proved to be just as extreme. The shoes favored by rich burghers were particularly wide and bulbous, and were therefore known derisively in Germany as "bear's paws," or "cow's-mouth" shoes. However, despite their almost square design, they were still rather uncomfortable, on the whole, compared with the poulaine. For one thing, the shoe was no longer fitted closely to the foot. Also, "cow's-mouth" shoes were made of a very rigid material consisting of several layers of leather, in extreme cases with two bulges that looked like horns at the toe, on account of which they were called "horned" shoes. This meant that the shoes were inflexible and did not accommodate the movements of the foot. One prominent feature of the Renaissance shoe was the slashes in the leather upper, which allowed the wearer's white stocking to show through as far as the toes. From 1565, the colorful Spanish shoe conquered Europe and made for rather more comfort with its soft material.

During the age of the baroque, men favored shoes made of the finest materials (leather or textiles like brocade) with high heels (see page 162) and extravagant decorations, such as ribbons tied in bows, large buckles, embroidered patterns, and jewels. The rococo, which developed in France under Louis XV (1715-1774), replaced the pomposity of baroque footwear with daintier, more elegant shoes.

Pattens (fifteenth century) were intended to give the poulaine support when walking and protect it against dirt (Bayerisches Nationalmuseum, Munich).

The art and fashion of this period were still strongly indebted to courtly traditions, but isolated new bourgeois influences can also be traced in the products of these years.

The boot gained new significance during the military conflicts that dominated the eighteenth century (the War of Spanish Succession, the wars against Turkey, and the American and French Revolutions, to name but a few). In addition to the very tight, elegant boots made of soft leather worn till then by courtiers (who had to dip their feet in water before they could even pull them on with the help of a servant), many people now began to wear strong boots with high shafts, which remained in use among the military until the end of the eighteenth century.

The intellectual model of modern men's fashion developed in the course of the emancipation of the bourgeoisie during the French Revolution (1789-1799). Bourgeois fashion reflected the central ideas of the revolution: equality and fraternity. From now on, powerful men stopped wearing shoes with extravagant decorations, colors and forms became more discreet, and the high heel disappeared completely. Hippolyte Taine (1828-1893), the French historian and philosopher, put forward the thesis that the invention of long pants that covered the ankle was the greatest event in European history because it created civilized man. We might add that in the process it brought into existence the forerunners of what we regard today as classic shoes, which went better with this style of pants.

Shoe designs adorned with ribbons and other such nostalgic decorations enjoyed a brief revival during the Biedermeier period and the rise of the Romantic movement in the early years of the nineteenth century, but since the middle of that century fashion in men's shoes has seen only occasional extreme alterations in style and has been primarily dominated by the classic shoe.

New styles of shoe and boot have found their place on the fashion scene from time to time, mainly thanks to trendsetting social figures and the military (the Wellington boot, for example, and the Blucher or Derby, see page 62). For a long time the ankle boot dominated

Louis XIV (1638-1715) depicted as the Sun King, wearing richly decorated shoes (Bibliothèque Nationale, Paris).

"Horned shoes" with horn-like bulges on the toe of the shoe were inflexible and did not accommodate the movements of the foot (Bayerisches Nationalmuseum, Munich).

footwear fashion. In this connection, one arbiter of fashion is particularly worthy of note, the Englishman George Bryan Brummel (1781-1840), better known as Beau Brummel. He favored matching colors, placed great emphasis on exactness of cut, and wore laced ankle boots with tightly fitting pants. His example was emulated by men in Great Britain, continental Europe, and elsewhere in the world until well into the twentieth century (among them friends and admirers such as the Prince Regent, who later became King George IV of England).

The styles still considered to be traditional classics were created with comfort and elegance in mind. More than anyone else, it was the master shoemakers of London, Munich, Paris, Vienna, and Budapest who contributed to the establishment of this conservative fashion.

The musician in *The Peasant Dance* by Pieter Breughel the Elder (painted *circa* 1568) wears the wide "cow's-mouth" shoes common at the time with white stockings (Kunsthistorisches Museum, Vienna).

Basic Types of Classic Men's Shoes

The basic types of men's shoes today regarded as classics were developed as the result of competition between the great European shoemakers during the years 1880-1889. The workshops of London, Paris, Munich, Vienna, and Budapest achieved fame around the world, thanks to their skillfulness and the individuality of their shoes.

A shoe is categorized primarily by the style of its construction as belonging to one of a few main groups. Shoe styles are first of all defined by the fastenings used as laced shoes (closed or open), buckle shoes, or slippers. On a closed lace-up shoe, such as the Oxford, the quarters are sewn under the vamp and fasten over the tongue, which is sewn onto the vamp. In the case of an open-lacing shoe, such as the Derby, the quarters lie over the vamp, which is made of the same piece of leather as the tongue. Another characteristic is the number of components making up the shoe upper. The upper of the simplest shoe, the slipper, consists of a single piece of leather. Styles like the Budapest consist of a vamp, quarters, and an outer counter. In addition, the vamp can be divided by a straight, or winged, toe cap, and various types of apron. The third way of identifying shoes is the presence, or absence, of patterns of punched perforations (brogueing), which have been a feature of fashionable men's shoes since the end of the nineteenth century.

There are less than a dozen basic classic shoe styles, but they offer limitless possibilities for variation when designing individual models. When deciding on the basic structure of the shoe, the designer will always draw on the traditional range of shoes. His creativity is allowed greater freedom when it comes to the design of the upper. How should the lines run? How will the different parts combine together harmoniously? Which types of decoration (brogueing, stitching, gimped edges, inlaid panels), colors, and textures are suitable, and what combinations are possible?

While shoemakers around the world are in agreement on the nomenclature of the basic types of shoe, the innumerable variations on these styles produced by the different workshops have individual names of their own. A selection of the styles that have been developed by famous workshops is given on pages 60-85.

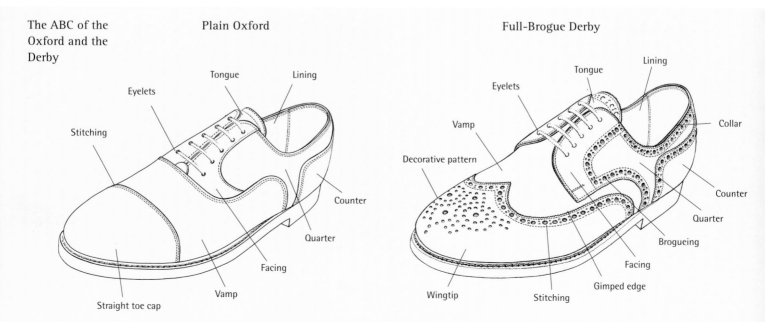

The ABC of the Oxford and the Derby

Plain Oxford

Full-Brogue Derby

The Full-brogue and Semi-brogue

The opposite of the puritanical plain Oxford is a richly decorated full-brogue – this is a perfect example from the workshop of Oliver Moore in New York.

The simplest early versions of the Oxford and the Derby bore no decoration at all, but shoemakers soon began to decorate the classic men's shoes with all sorts of ornamentation. It was Irish farmers who first began to decorate shoes with patterns of holes. Their shoes tended to become waterlogged due to the wet ground in the bogs where they worked. They put holes into the toe caps and quarters of their heavy leather shoes so that the insides would dry better.

In England this type of shoe first became popular with foresters and gamekeepers, then later among the aristocratic circles who went hunting in their company. Once the brogue had found its way into the closets of the nobility, it went through a process of transformation. Shoemakers began to make brogues out of ever softer and thinner leather, and the lines became markedly more elegant. The original function of the perforations (brogueing) was forgotten; they were now purely decorative features. The pattern of holes on the toe of the shoe became much more delicate, the joins between the vamp and the quarters, and the upper edge, or top line, of the quarters, were decorated with brogueing and edged with stitching. The result was the creation of the full-brogue and the semi-brogue (also known as the half-brogue). The only difference between the full-brogue and the semi-brogue is the shape of the toe cap, which is winged on a full-brogue and straight on a semi-brogue. (See pages 106 ff. for the techniques used to make brogueing and other types of pattern.)

Full-brogue shoes were already to be seen on golf courses in England at the beginning of the twentieth century - they were regarded as a kind of sports shoe. They only found massive popularity around the world when the Prince of Wales, who was regarded in the 1930s as the most elegant man in Europe, astonished society by wearing full-brogues to play golf. He was so fond of brogue shoes that he also liked to wear a more elegant version on social occasions.

Despite the example given by the Prince of Wales, semi-brogues and full-brogues are still not worn after six o'clock in the evening.

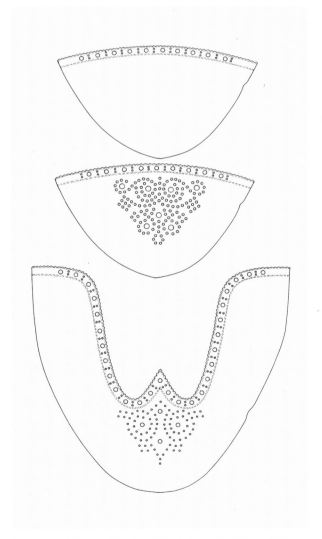

Three different toe caps. Top: plain. Center: straight with decorative pattern (semi-brogue). Bottom: winged with decorative pattern (full-brogue).

The Oxford

The Oxford is by far the most elegant English men's shoe and is to be recognized by its closed lacing. The laces are threaded through five pairs of eyelets and fasten up the shoe so perfectly that only the upper edge of the tongue can be seen. This type of shoe looks particularly good on narrow feet with a low instep.

Because the pants form a continuation of the shoe, it is vitally important that the two are in harmony. The combination of a black suit with a pair of black Oxfords guarantees the wearer a distinguished appearance on formal and festive occasions. Together with plain pants, it shows good taste in everyday situations, as exemplified here by the famous dancer and film star Fred Astaire while attending an unconventional autograph-signing session.

The Oxford is regarded as a characteristically English shoe. Shoes of this type were being made in England as early as 1830, but first came into fashion around 1880, and have been widely known as Oxfords ever since. The prototype of the modern Oxford was made in the workshop of John Lobb about 100 years ago. It is still considered to be the most elegant style of men's shoe.

Oxfords on parade. Left: a smooth plain Oxford; the only decoration on this elegant, highly ascetic shoe is the double seam along the straight toe cap and the join between the vamp and the quarters. Center: a semi-brogue; the straight toe cap, the seams joining the toe cap and the quarters, and the quarters and the counter, as well as the ones along the bottom of the facings and the top line of the quarters, are all decorated with brogueing. Right: a typical full-brogue with a richly decorated wingtip in classic style.
(Unless otherwise indicated, all the shoes shown in this chapter were made at the workshops of L. Vass in Budapest.)

The Derby

The Derby is a shoe with open lacing much worn in continental Europe. Shoes with lacing of this kind are also known as "Bluchers" after the Prussian field marshal Gebhard Leberecht von Blücher, Duke of Wahlstadt (1742-1819), who joined forces with Wellington to defeat Napoleon at the Battle of Waterloo in 1815 and ordered laced shoes of this type to be made for his soldiers.

The Derby offers pure comfort to shoe-lovers who have a wide foot or an unusually high instep. At the same time, the decorations soften the character of the shoe, which looks particularly robust on account of its top seams (on lock-stitched versions) and the built-up sole. The open lacing means that it is easier to slip into this shoe than an Oxford, and the distance between the two quarters is easier to adjust. Derbys are available in many different styles: plain, semi-brogue, and full-brogue.

This shoe style has been popular since the beginning of the twentieth century, particularly in Vienna. It can be characterized as being cut like a Derby and decorated as a semi-brogue. The vamp is divided 3 inches [7-8 cm] from the tip of the shoe by a straight toe cap decorated with a series of holes between two seams. The pattern is made up of a row of large holes with pairs of smaller holes placed side by side in the gaps between them. The decorative patterning on the toe cap is dominated by large holes surrounded by a ring of smaller ones. The brogueing between the two seams is repeated on the vamp, quarters, and counter.

A plain Derby looks almost puritanical. Its vamp is not divided, the quarter falls down to the sole in a single smooth curve. Many shoe-lovers prefer this simple style to a semi-brogue or full-brogue out of a completely unfounded fear that straight, or winged, toe caps could cramp their feet and be uncomfortable. Scotch-grain leather (left) emphasizes the relaxed, casual nature of the shoe.

André Kostolányi, a Hungarian by birth, makes his living trading in stocks and shares and lives in Paris and Munich. He does not just wear bespoke Derbys: "I have been wearing bespoke shoes since my earliest boyhood because my grandfather and father wore them in old Budapest. This used to be more natural in bourgeois circles than it is today. For me, personally, a good shoe has always been more important for judging a real gentleman than his suit. In 1924 I was even caught up in a scandal in France on account of a pair of shoes. I met a member of the Vanderbilt family at the Casino in Deauville. My friend was so daring as to wear yellow shoes with a black tuxedo: and this was a scandal for the Parisian society press. As far as I am concerned, the state of the shoe industry and footwear trade is always an important indicator of the general consumer climate. If there are plenty of shoes being bought, other sectors of the economy are also doing well."

Whatever the color, whether semi-brogue or full-brogue, the Derby is a shoe that can be worn till the sun goes down. With a matching suit, every shade of brown is appropriate at meetings and in the office. Worsted or moleskin trousers underline the casual character of the shoe. It is also ideal leisurewear with jeans in summer and cord pants in winter. Combined with a black, dark-blue, or dark-gray suit, plain black Derbys can compete with the elegance of the Oxford at any festive occasion or simply as evening wear. As can be seen, there is no limit to the range of designs possible for the classic Derby.

A shoe that provokes contradictory emotions. Some people love it and cannot bear to be without a pair in their personal shoe collection. Others never take to it. The Norwegian shoe is a variant of the basic Derby characterized by an unusual division of the vamp and hand stitching on the upper. One seam runs at a height of about 1 inch [2.5 cm] parallel to the edge of the sole, the other runs vertically down to the sole at the tip of the shoe. The leather edges are turned outward and sewn together precisely and carefully by hand. By comparison with classic shoes, even the most elegant Norwegian looks casual. The rustic character of this shoe is usually emphasized even more by the choice of materials. It is particularly popular in grained leather and often made in contrasting, sometimes startling, colors. An extravagant shoe that represents a youthful challenge to the shoemaker.

This Derby is an example of modern design and refined understatement. In contrast to the familiar curve of the Derby, the quarters are laid over the smooth vamp, and, instead of the traditional four to six pairs of eyelets, there is a single pair. The whole upper radiates perfect harmony: a shoe made by the Berluti workshop in Paris.

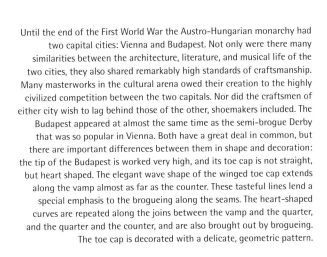

Until the end of the First World War the Austro-Hungarian monarchy had two capital cities: Vienna and Budapest. Not only were there many similarities between the architecture, literature, and musical life of the two cities, they also shared remarkably high standards of craftsmanship. Many masterworks in the cultural arena owed their creation to the highly civilized competition between the two capitals. Nor did the craftsmen of either city wish to lag behind those of the other, shoemakers included. The Budapest appeared at almost the same time as the semi-brogue Derby that was so popular in Vienna. Both have a great deal in common, but there are important differences between them in shape and decoration: the tip of the Budapest is worked very high, and its toe cap is not straight, but heart shaped. The elegant wave shape of the winged toe cap extends along the vamp almost as far as the counter. These tasteful lines lend a special emphasis to the brogueing along the seams. The heart-shaped curves are repeated along the joins between the vamp and the quarter, and the quarter and the counter, and are also brought out by brogueing. The toe cap is decorated with a delicate, geometric pattern.

The Monk

The Monk (so called because it is reminiscent of the sandals worn by monks) is an independent style of shoe. It consists of a vamp and quarters, like the Oxford and the Derby, but differs from them markedly in that the two quarters are fastened together with a distinctive buckle. The buckle is fastened to one of the quarters, while the other ends in a leather strap, which is threaded through the buckle and used to adjust the distance between the quarters across the instep. Most Monks have an undivided smooth vamp on which the buckle and the strap stand out to full effect. The buckles themselves vary greatly, and can be silver or golden, square or round, and have smooth or patterned surfaces. The advantage of the Monk is the simplicity of its buckle fastening. This contrasts with the Derby, for example, with its complicated lacing, which leaves the ends of the laces lying on the shoe.

This plain Monk is very similar to a plain Derby. The only difference is the buckle, which fastens the quarters together instead of two or three eyelets. It is the long vamp that lends this shoe its air of elegance.

This shoe, which dates from the end of the nineteenth century, is both something of a curiosity and a real treat for the eyes. It was designed to go with Scottish folk costume as a dance shoe worn with a kilt. While the Monk is generally dominated by a rather puritanical simplicity, this shoe from the workshop of John Lobb in London is covered with rich decorations. It is a remarkable variation on the full-brogue, not just the front of the vamp, which is divided by a winged toe cap, but the sides and even the counter are covered in luxuriant brogueing. The division of the vamp is also interesting: the apron and the quarters have been made out of a single piece of leather. The characteristic buckle plays a subordinate role.

This variant with two buckles is very popular among real Monk-lovers. The vamp of the shoe shown here is divided by a straight toe cap. However, its real decoration comes in the shape of the two decorative buckles and the quarter that ends in two straps that are laid over the tongue and cover the instep almost completely.
This shoe was made by John Lobb in Paris.

A Monk can be classically elegant or casual and relaxed. The most popular black, plain Monk is ideal footwear for the businessman. If his pants are long enough no one will be able to see whether he is wearing plain Derbys or buckled Monks. In other shades this shoe is worn with casual day clothes, such as pants and a sweater.

The Slipper

The slipper is a light, flexible shoe made of soft leather with a thin sole. Slippers are so comfortable that the wearer is hardly aware of them on his feet. They go perfectly with a casual look. In addition to its simple original form, the slipper (also known as the loafer) is found in a welted version. The advantages of the slipper were raised to new heights in 1979 when Diego Della Valle introduced his J.P. Tod's onto the market. This driving shoe with small rubber studs embedded in its sole is a real moccasin. Della Valle removed all the hard leather from the sole and the inner, and had the sole and the upper made of a single piece of leather.

The moccasin worn by the American Indians was the predecessor of this shoe. It is known as the "slipper" because all you have to do is slip your foot into it. The vamp, the quarters, and the tongue are made of a single piece of leather, and it has no laces or buckles. However, while the sole of the moccasin is made of very thin, flexible leather, the slipper is similar in construction to the classic shoe styles described above. The common decorative elements used on slippers include hand-stitched aprons and tassels attached to the tongue. The overall effect is one of casual elegance, well befitting a gentleman's wardrobe.

J.P. Tod's are "hand made in Italy." The American film star Michael Douglas wears these moccasins, the precursors of the classic slipper, in appropriate surroundings as he takes it easy on the beach, a rare moment of relaxation during the making of a film.

In essence, the Penny Loafer is a type of slipper. Its distinguishing feature is the decorative leather bar laid across the tongue. A penny piece used to be slipped under this bar – hence the name of the style. The curves of the leather bar can be varied in countless ways, adding attractive detail to the classic design.

The leather tassels found on many slippers have the disadvantage that they easily get caught in the seams of the wearer's pants. For this reason many customers order their bespoke slippers without tassels.

It is the leather alone that makes a summer shoe of this Oxford, with its classic lines. The Bálint workshop in Vienna ordered the leather to be finished particularly soft and not dyed after tanning, but left with its natural color.

Summer Shoes

As a matter of principle, all the classic shoe styles can be turned into air-permeable summer shoes if the shoemaker selects a thin leather or inserts woven leather at certain points in the upper. Summer shoes manufactured according to the strict rules of classic shoemaking are therefore by no means only intended for one season. In a European climate they will last much longer than a machine-worked pair, which can only be worn for a few months in many cases.

Surprisingly enough, summer shoes are more often made in dark colors than light ones. Someone wearing black, or dark-blue, Derbys with a woven vamp at a wedding will not be bothered by the heat. A pair of Derbys with large perforations or sandals would certainly be quite inappropriate for such an occasion, though both offer comfort on hot summer days and are ideal for informal parties in the open air.

The Russian composer Igor Stravinsky (here shown in Venice in 1951) loved improvisation, but not when it came to shoes. In this area he was a stickler for tradition.

This classic Derby is decorated with a woven vamp that forms a startling contrast to its smooth quarters. Woven leather is much more air permeable than the thinnest plain leather. A sheet of leather is cut into strips about an eighth of an inch [3-5 mm] wide, and some of the leather strips are hung parallel to each other on a construction rather like a loom. The shoemaker then threads the remaining strips through at right angles, running them over and under the hanging strips in an alternating pattern (in fact, he weaves the leather). This creates a woven leather surface with a pattern of squares - the narrower the strips, the more attractive will be the final appearance of the shoe.

Holes punched in the leather guarantee total air permeability. The toe and facings of this Derby are smooth, but all the other parts have been decorated with relatively large holes. On the one hand, these have a similar esthetic function to brogueing; on the other, they ensure that air circulates and the shoe is pleasantly cool. The holes are arranged in a systematic geometric pattern laid down by the designer. Holes of an eighth of an inch [3 mm] diameter are placed five-eighths of an inch [1.5 cm] apart in a kind of network. The upper leather and the lining of this summer shoe are punched through in the same places. The lining is needed to give the upper support, as in most shoes.

Unlike their ancient predecessors, modern sandals are not status symbols by any means. They are worn above all for comfort because they are the coolest things to wear in very hot weather. This sandal retains several easily recognizable elements of the classic men's shoe. The toe is plain and the counter hidden, allowing the bars of different widths to stand out more effectively, particularly the one that runs right over the top of the instep. This sandal is a typical variation on the Monk. The quarter is extended into a strap, which fastens with a buckle. In this case, practicality was uppermost in the designer's mind. At the same time, he created something special with the simplicity of his design, giving sophistication to a casual shoe.

Boots

Our feet need greater protection in cold winters. This is provided by boots, principally by the quarters, which extend 2-4 inches [5-10 cm] above the ankle. Boots do not just cover the foot but also the lower parts of the leg. Both the Oxford and the Derby are available as boots in plain, semi-brogue, and full-brogue styles.

The same materials and techniques are used as when making shoes. The only difference is that the soles of boots are built up, often with a rubber outsole to prevent slipping in snow or on wet ground. The quarters can be fastened using eyelets, eyes, or buttons. As the pants cover the quarters almost completely, boots can be matched with the same outfits as shoes. However, they should not be worn on special occasions, for which classic shoes should be reserved.

Ankle boots came into fashion in England around 1840. This one was made by Zak in Vienna.

This semi-brogue Derby is a popular variant on the winter boot. Its lacing is of particular interest. The laces are first threaded through two pairs of eyelets, as on a normal shoe, then drawn higher through a series of eyes.

The forerunner of this boot, known as the Balmoral, was made for Prince Albert in the middle of the nineteenth century by J. Sparkes Hall, Queen Victoria's shoemaker, when the royal couple went to Scotland for a long holiday at Balmoral Castle. Several decades later this plain Oxford with its high quarters and long laces was part of the everyday footwear worn by both men and women.

It is possible for designers to vary the plain Oxford boot in many ways: its basic shape is derived from classic traditions, but can be combined with daring innovations to great effect.

The quarters of this boot have been cut in an elegant curve and are sewn together in the middle. The laces threaded crosswise through ten pairs of eyes are the only decoration on this product of the Bertl workshop in Munich, but all the more outstanding for that.

The Design

At one time the designer would first make a detailed, realistic drawing, which usually showed the shoe from several different angles. Today he is increasingly more likely to draw the parts of the shoe upper and their decoration directly onto the last. This creates a design in three dimensions, which is much more practical for working purposes.

This method has other advantages. It is easier to check that the decorations and proportions – of the toe cap, quarters, and counter, for example – are correct. If the designer is not happy with what he has drawn, he can always rub out a line that does not fit, or even the entire design, and begin again. At this early stage in the design process, it is usual for a new design to be shown to everyone working in a workshop.

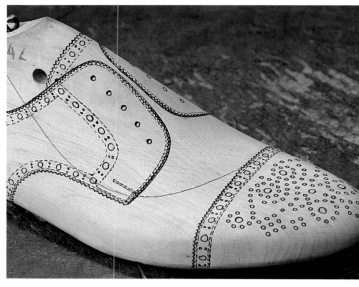

Semi-brogue Derby

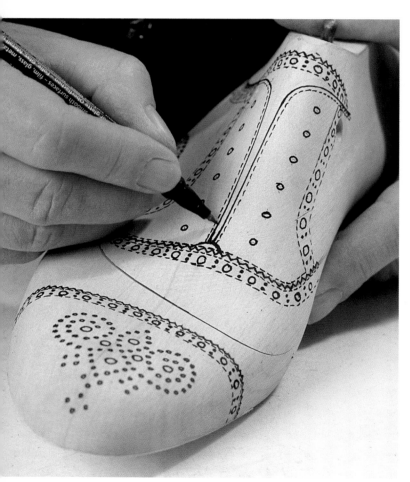

Semi-brogue Oxford   Plain Oxford

Plain Derby

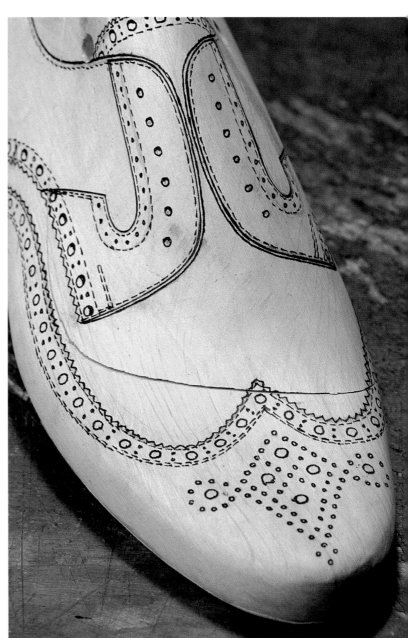

Full-brogue Derby

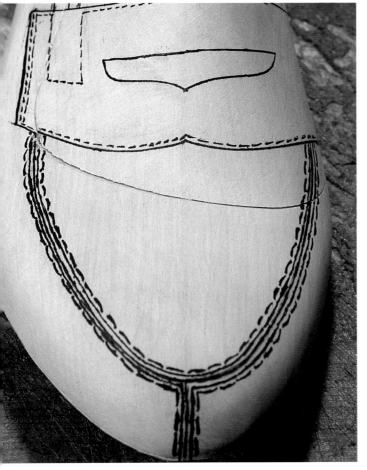

Penny Loafer

The Form

The shoe designer then copies his design from the last onto a piece of paper because the design he has drawn now needs to be laid out in two dimensions in order to create the basic pattern from which the parts of the upper are cut, the "form."

Experienced shoemakers are of the opinion that it is possible to create a sufficiently precise form from the three-dimensional last using a pencil, some paper, a sharp knife, a measuring tape, and a few tacks.

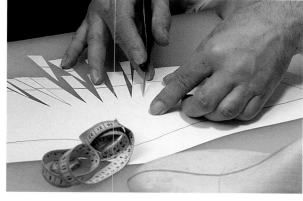

After the silhouette of the last has been cut out roughly, the shoemaker cuts slots into the paper along the center line.

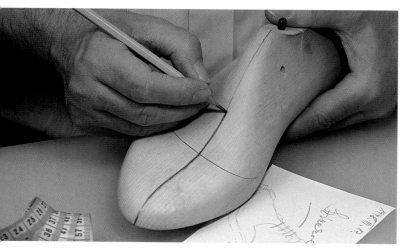

First of all, the center line of the last is drawn in from the tip of the toe to the bottom of the heel. This ensures that the two parts of the form are of the same size.

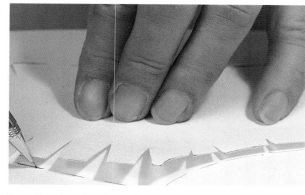

The outline of the slotted paper is copied onto another piece of paper. An allowance of about three-quarters of an inch [1.5-2 cm] (the amount of upper leather usually tacked onto the last) is added under the sole line. The form for the upper is now complete.

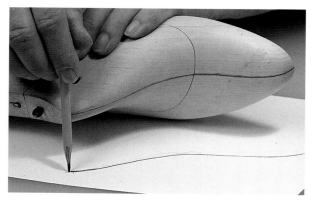

Next the last is laid with its outer side on the paper, the silhouette traced with a pencil, and the pattern cut out, making a small allowance in each case for good measure.

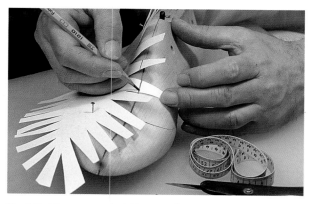

The slotted form can now be laid more easily round the last. The shoemaker tacks the paper firmly into place and copies the essential features of the design onto it, as can be seen in the photograph.

Typical Forms

All the lines, curves, and decorative elements that have been drawn on the last are copied precisely onto the form. Every feature can be identified clearly and easily: how many pieces the upper is made of, where and how the parts fit together, the size of the decorative elements, and how they relate to each other. The dimensions and shape of the form match those of the customer's foot. It is now used to make a series of what are known as "working patterns" for the separate components of which the upper

consists (as many as seven patterns, depending on the particular model).

The working patterns and the form are marked with the customer's name and sent to the clickers in a small bag. They are used by the clicker to cut the upper parts out of the required leather in the selected color. The closer assembles them and adds the decorations shown on the form. Finally, the various parts of the upper are stitched together (see pages 106 ff.).

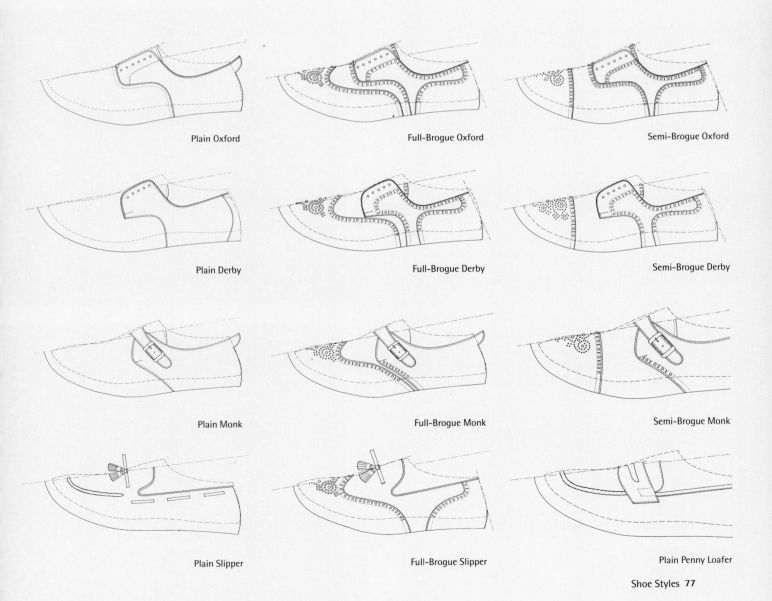

| Plain Oxford | Full-Brogue Oxford | Semi-Brogue Oxford |

| Plain Derby | Full-Brogue Derby | Semi-Brogue Derby |

| Plain Monk | Full-Brogue Monk | Semi-Brogue Monk |

| Plain Slipper | Full-Brogue Slipper | Plain Penny Loafer |

A Choice of Colors

The history of men's shoe fashion has not just been dominated by characteristic styles, but by particular colors. The accounts and pictures that have been passed down to us show that during certain periods men's shoes were very colorful indeed. Depending on fashion or the wearer's rank, they might be silver, gold, red, violet, or even canary yellow. The high point of magnificent coloring, the baroque, has already been mentioned at the beginning of this chapter.

Ever since the classic hand-sewn shoes came into existence, not only have their shapes been remarkably constant, but also the range of unostentatious colors felt to be appropriate to them. At times one is tempted to think that men's shoes are only allowed in two colors: black and brown. This may not be true, but the selection of subdued conventional colors is relatively narrow, even if the opportunities offered by different shades of color and their combinations with different surface finishes are unusually rich.

If we mix the six colors of the spectrum - red, orange, yellow, green, blue, and violet - with black, the products are what are known as dark colors, the most popular colors for men's shoes, alongside black. Several hundred different gradations of these dark colors are available: brown, for example, runs from a dark brown that looks almost black to tan and light tan. The red scale is also very finely graduated: from cherry red to Bordeaux and bull's blood.

The color of the individual shoe can never be considered in isolation. It always creates an effect in combination with the colors of the wearer's clothes: his suit - or combination of jacket and pants - his shirt, necktie, and socks. There are a number of unwritten laws that have to be followed when assembling an outfit. For instance, it is obligatory for a man to wear shiny black shoes with a black suit. Dark-brown and light-tan shoes go with brown suits, and can be used to vary the entire effect of an outfit. Gray pants combine well with black, dark-blue, green, Bordeaux, and even cherry-red shoes. If at all possible, socks should be chosen in the same shade as the shoes. The harmony of colors created by these basic rules will be recognized as an expression of good taste, and no matter where you are or what the occasion, your footwear will not let you down.

Combining Colors and Leathers

The traditional plain shoe is still regarded as "gentlemanlike," but shoemakers and designers keep trying to overcome the dull respectability of the classic colors by using various combinations of colors and leathers in the shoe upper. Even the simplest version of the plain Oxford offers opportunities for this sort of variation, not to mention uppers with more parts.

However, as a rule, shoe designers restrict themselves to combinations of two colors or contrasting leather finishes. Any more than this would be regarded as excessive extravagance.

The combination of two shades of the same color, such as medium and dark brown, represents a modest challenge to the authority of tradition. Much more daring is the combination of completely different colors, such as brown and Bordeaux, black and tan, black and Bordeaux, or black and brown - just to mention a few of the numerous possibilities.

A designer can also create amazing contrasts by combining leathers with different surface textures -

smooth and grained, for example. However, combinations of this type must respect the strict unwritten rule that the tip of the shoe has to be of smooth leather so that it can always be polished to a bright shine or, if the shoe is a full-brogue, that nothing detracts from the decorative pattern.

Of course, when designing a bespoke shoe, the designer and the shoemaker work hand in hand with the customer. Again, as when taking the foot measurements, it is essential for an intensive discussion to take place so that the designer and the shoemaker have as much information as possible about the various occasions on which the customer wants to wear the shoes, and are able to acquaint themselves with his personal style. Only in this way can they give good advice and unite his individual wishes successfully with their professional experience. The importance of this understanding between customer and designer and shoemaker cannot be overemphasized, as it is this that will ensure true elegance and style.

This full-brogue Oxford is a perfect example of a very ambitious combination of colors and leathers. It is the contrast between the smooth, shiny vamp, facings, and counter; and the matte, silky quarters and apron that makes this shoe from the workshop of John Lobb in London so beautiful.

This full-brogue Derby combines textured Scotch grain and leather with a smooth finish.

Golf Shoes

Special clothing is needed in order to play any sport to the highest level. Although ordinary shoes were quite sufficient for tennis, fencing, cricket, and golf in their early days, specialized footwear soon developed, particularly in these sports.

Golf shoes are based on the full-brogue Derby. On account of the conditions of the sport in question - golf is played out of doors and mostly on grass - shoemakers began to use heavy, weatherproof leather for the vamp and the quarters, usually strong Scotch grain in dark shades. The apron is generally made of a softer leather, often in white.

With regard to shape, construction, cut, and manufacturing methods, the golf shoe is similar to the black and white Budapest on the next page, though there are significant differences. One feature distinguishing the golf shoe is the large tongue decorated with tassels and brogueing, which is laid over the vamp after the shoes have been laced in order to protect the laces from damp. Another is the spikes, which are screwed into the sole and the heel (four in the heel, five to seven in the sole) to give the player's feet a better grip on the turf. Golf shoes are usually sold with two different, easily exchanged, sets of spikes; one for soft conditions, the other for hard ground.

Most golf shoes are bespoke shoes. As a rule, professional golfers own two pairs, one for training and the other, more lavishly decorated, for competitions.

This golf shoe, a full-brogue Derby, is an unusual combination of textured Scotch grain and smooth leather, and contrasting white and green sections. A replacement tongue in the same green as the vamp is provided with this shoe made by Bálint of Vienna so that the wearer can change the tongue during play if it has become wet or dirty. At first sight it looks as though he is wearing a new pair of shoes!

Contrasting Colors: Black and White

Black and white: the most perfect and, at the same time, the most extreme contrast in the world of colors. Despite this, where shoes are concerned, it has been a symbol for togetherness and identification ever since the age of jazz: a combination of colors with ideological content.

In the early years of the twentieth century a new musical style characterized by tempered scales and a hard, brash sound was created in the United States as a result of the fusion of European and African elements. During the 1920s jazz emerged from the ghetto to which it was confined as a form of folk music and achieved global success, making a huge impact on mass entertainment and culture in the first half of the twentieth century. Nor were the famous fashion companies able to escape its influence. Jazz style dominated New York and the European fashion centers. It was daring and casual, and summed up the free, unconstrained spirit of the times. The new kind of music brought all races closer together, whether on the stage or in the audience. In the same way, the musicians and, later, the film stars of Hollywood were also able to express their human solidarity when they wore the Spectator, a classic shoe in contrasting colors popular in these circles. Jazz style gained many adherents: Al Capone, the Prince of Wales, Gene Kelly, Fred Astaire, and Louis Armstrong all wore this shoe. In essence, the Spectator is a black shoe, and usually it is only the apron, the vamp, or the quarters that are made of white leather, making the contrast.

The semi-brogue Oxford Spectator was a favorite among the great jazz musicians of the USA in the 20s and 30s.

The glory days of the Spectator were during the years between 1920 and 1930, but it is still revived from time to time. Today it can be seen at receptions and similar festive occasions, and is worn with a matching suit.

This full-brogue Derby shows that Budapests are just as elegant in black and white.

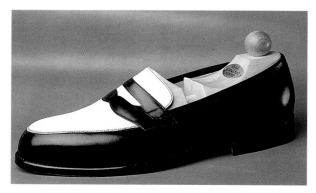

The contrast of colors is intensified by the strips of the decorative bar on this Penny Loafer.

Even the Balmoral boot can be made in black and white. This example comes from the Bertl workshop in Munich.

The Spectator was part of the everyday clothing worn by stylish young dandies during the 1920s and 1930s. Today it embodies a feeling of nostalgia for times past. It lends its wearer an extravagant appearance at any time of the day or night, and goes well with suits or pants of all colors (except brown). However, if you really want to bring back the elegance of the jazz age, wear Spectators with a white suit or a combination of white jacket and black pants. Young people first became enthusiastic about this two-tone combination during the 1950s. The couple shown in this photograph are wearing an American classic: the saddle shoe for the jazz-dance party. These shoes have white vamps and quarters, and extremely large black facings that reach down to the sole.

The Upper

Leather

The elegance and durability of a shoe depend to a crucial extent on the quality of the materials used. In consequence, the first rule of shoemaking is to exercise great care when selecting the leather for the upper and the sole of the shoe.

Animal leather is still the most suitable material for the manufacture of shoes because it provides the foot with lasting protection against injury as well as adverse weather conditions, and it is also air permeable and extremely easy to work.

The skins of many animals can be used to make shoe uppers: cattle (cows, bulls, oxen, calves), horses, goats, deer, and also - just to mention a few of the more exotic possibilities - elephants, crocodiles, lizards, and fish, as well as ostrich, turkey, and goose legs.

Since the beginning of the twentieth century most hand-sewn men's shoes have been made of calfskin, cowhide, or horse leather. In recent years kangaroo has become more common, but exotic leathers are still used comparatively rarely.

The upper of this full-brogue Oxford is made of leather that was first tanned 200 years ago. In 1973 divers from the nautical archeology section of a sub-aqua club based in Plymouth found a ship's bell at a depth of 100 feet [30 m] in Plymouth Sound on the south coast of England. They had discovered the wreck of the *Frau Metta Catharina*, which had capsized in Plymouth Sound during a storm in December 1786 (see map for location of wreck). Its cargo was bundles of vegetable-tanned reindeer skins from St. Petersburg. After a short process of restoration these skins were suitable again for making shoes and were used by several shoemakers, including Klemann (Basthorst, Germany), where the bespoke men's shoe shown here was created. (Map by Craig Bramwell based on an original dating from eighteenth century, published in G. Garbett and I. Skelton, *The Wreck of the Metta Catharina*, New Pages: Pulla Cross, Truro, England.)

Animal skins consist of three clearly distinguishable layers: the outer layer of skin, or epidermis, the fibrous inner layer, or corium, and the subcutaneous connective tissues, known as the flesh. The most valuable layer is the corium, which is used to make shoe uppers, soles, and various other accessories, as well as products not connected with the footwear trade. The corium has to be separated from the epidermis and the flesh during the preparation of raw skins and hides.

Raw skins and hides are conserved by cooling (mainly in countries with cold climates), drying (mainly in warm regions), or salting. All three procedures are effective ways to prevent skins and hides from decaying.

As early as the Stone Age humans discovered various uses for leather and tried to find ways of making it flexible, hard-wearing, and durable. In some cases, skins were preserved simply by drying, but this was never a real success: they became fragile in the sun and quickly decayed in damp conditions. Another, no more successful, approach was to conserve skins by scraping off the flesh layer and pounding and beating them intensively. A decisive development came when it was realized that the hair could be removed from skins more effectively with ash and quick lime, or by smoking (a technique known as smoke tanning). Chamois tanning, in which the leather is tanned with fats and oils, has been practiced since as long ago as *circa* 6000 BC. One of the prehistoric tanning methods is still used today by Eskimos, who chew animal skins, then rub fat into them once they have been softened with saliva.

The craft of tanning has always been closely associated with shoemaking. The earliest evidence we have about the trade comes from Egyptian wall paintings. In Egypt, as in Ancient Greece and Rome, the most common preservation techniques were vegetable tanning (using spruce, oak, and alder bark, or the skins of oakgall, pomegranates, and acorns) and chamois tanning. Expensive leather was tanned with alum (a mineral salt), which colored it white. This mineral-tanning technique is probably among the oldest methods of preparing leather. Alum made the leather rigid, and it had to be stretched later before it could be worked.

Whether vegetable, chamois, or mineral tanning, the essential features of the main tanning procedures have not changed to the present day. Just like the art of shoemaking, the craft of the modern tanner has a history and tradition going back thousands of years.

The raw skins are conserved by salting to prevent them from decaying.

Preparation for Tanning

Even today the methods used to prepare raw skins and hides for tanning are based on discoveries made long ago. Across the whole industry, from small workshops working in a traditional fashion to the most advanced modern factories, production methods have remained essentially the same.

The actual "leather," the corium, consists of a network of fibers that form two distinct layers, one fine and one coarse. It is even possible to distinguish these two layers in cross section with the naked eye. The fine upper layer is the grain layer, which has hair shafts and the excretory ducts of the sebaceous and sweat glands running through it. Every leather possesses its own characteristic grain that gives it its uniquely attractive character. The lower layer is known as the flesh layer. This consists of innumerable crisscrossing bundles of fibers that give the leather its durability and hard-wearing qualities. The ratio between the grain and flesh layers of cowhide is 1 : 3.5, which makes it a hard-wearing leather that is ideal for tough working shoes, and it is not surprising that this type of leather is used so much.

The corium consists of up to 90% protein, mostly collagen. It is the properties of this substance that the tanner relies on during the preparation of skins and hides: collagen molecules absorb water easily and bind the various tanning materials.

The first step in the tanning process is to soften the raw skins in barrels or tubs of water. This removes dirt and preservatives (salt, for example) from the surface of the raw skin and restores its original fluid content.

In ancient and medieval times raw skins were stored in warm, damp conditions in order to make unhairing easier. The modern method, known as liming, is also traditional: the raw skins rest for 20-24 hours in barrels, tubs, or drums filled with a lime solution. This softens the epidermis and the flesh layers thoroughly.

Next, the flesh is removed from the raw skin. Machines have now taken over what was once extremely laborious manual labor. First, the subcutaneous connective tissue is removed from the raw skin softened with lime, revealing the flesh side of the corium. Then the skin is fed through knife cylinders to remove the epidermis, uncovering the grain side of the corium.

In order to make sure that both surfaces are as clean as possible after machine cleaning, the same procedures are carried out again by hand. The tanner uses a bent knife with two handles called a fleshing iron. This instrument has been in use among tanners for hundreds of years and looks similar to the tool that is used to shape the last.

Finally, the cleaned skin is checked thoroughly and graded carefully. It now becomes possible to judge the real quality of the skin. Only immaculate skins and hides are allowed through for further processing.

Assuming the inspection shows that the skin has no inperfections that would mean its rejection, it is now almost ready for the actual tanning process, (see page 93).

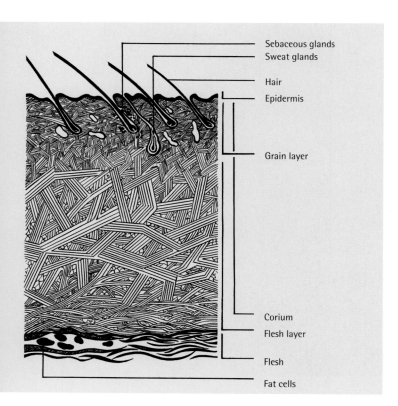

Sebaceous glands
Sweat glands

Hair
Epidermis

Grain layer

Corium

Flesh layer

Flesh

Fat cells

Animal skin is made up of proteins, water, fats, and minerals. Only one of its three layers can be used for leather manufacture: the corium, which divides into a grain layer and a flesh layer. The complex structure of the flesh layer, with bundles of fibers running in different directions, gives leather its unique strength.

The epidermis and flesh are softened in a lime solution.

Sharp knife cylinders remove the softened epidermis.

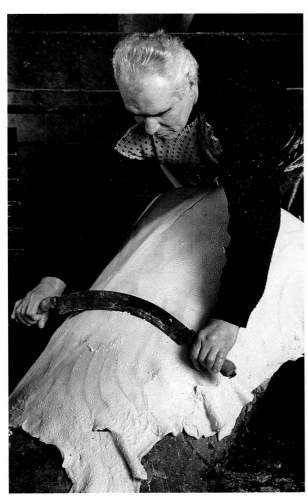
The surface is cleaned again with a fleshing iron.

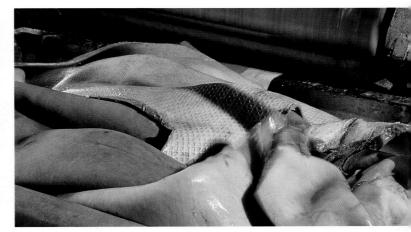
The cleaned skin is ready for tanning.

The skin is subject to a meticulous quality check before tanning.

Chrome-salt tanning makes leather soft, pleasant to the touch, flexible, heat-resistant, and easy to dye.

Tanning

The skins go through two more procedures before the actual tanning process. First of all, the lime solution is neutralized with various acids - hydrochloric acid, sulfuric acid, or lactic acid - and washed out with water. The skins are softened further by "bating," the aim of which is to loosen the fiber structure of the skin as much as possible so that it absorbs the tannage easily. This used to be done by covering the skin or hide with dog dung or the droppings of birds, such as chickens, but modern tanners use enzymes that degrade the proteins in the skin. Skins and hides are usually about a quarter inch [5-8 mm] thick when they arrive at the tannery. The tanner divides them into several sheets, or "splits." After further processing, the most valuable layer, the grain layer, is used for the upper leather of shoes. The grain layer is a fiftieth to a twentieth of an inch [0.6-1.8 mm] thick. In most cases, the leather in the upper of the shoe needs to be a twenty-fifth of an inch [1.2 mm] thick. The layer beneath it, the flesh layer, is used for linings, which are made in a similar thickness.

Next comes the most important process of all: tanning. Tanned leather differs from raw skin and hide in many ways. It does not become fragile and stiff if it comes into contact with water; it does not decay when wet, and dries again afterward; and it does not become glutinous if exposed to strong heat. The durability of the leather depends on the effectiveness of the tanning. This therefore has a decisive influence on the quality of the finished shoe and the wellbeing of the wearer's feet. Another important consideration that must not be neglected is the testing treatment that the leather will be exposed to as the shoe is built. It is tacked, stretched, blocked, and softened and must maintain its positive characteristics - its elasticity, strength, softness, and air permeability - throughout.

Until the middle of the nineteenth century the leathers used as shoe uppers and soles were made resistant, durable, and elastic mainly with vegetable materials (oak or spruce bark, chestnut wood, sumach leaves, and oakgall). Vegetable-tanned leather is easily recognized by its yellow or light-beige coloration. This procedure, vegetable tanning, is still used for the preparation of sole and lining leather.

As discussed above, apart from vegetable tanning, the Ancient Egyptians were also familiar with a form of mineral tanning. This mainly involved the use of alum and cooking salt. Modern mineral tanning, chrome-salt tanning, became widespread after 1858, when the German chemist Friedrich L. Knapp discovered the tanning properties of chrome salts. Since then this procedure has replaced vegetable tanning almost completely for certain types of leather (calfskin, cowhide, and horse leather). Most shoe uppers are made of chrome-tanned leather, as it is considerably softer and pleasanter to the touch, lighter, more flexible, more heat-resistant, and easier to dye than alum or vegetable-tanned leather. In addition, one great advantage of chrome-salt tanning is the time factor: it shortens the entire tanning process to six or seven weeks, compared to the six or seven months required previously.

In chrome-salt tanning the skins are placed in rotating drums filled with tanning liquor for 6-12 hours so that the chrome salts penetrate the skin from all directions. After tanning, the leather has to rest for at least 24 hours so that the structural changes that have taken place can fix effectively and completely in all the fibers.

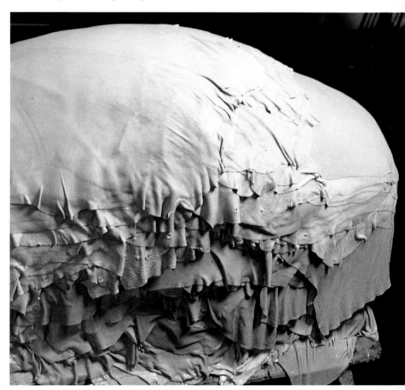

Skins tanned with chrome salts have a characteristic bluish color, whereas vegetable-tanned leather is yellowish.

The dyed leather is shown here being dried with infrared heaters.

An ancient method of drying leather on wooden frames.

Most box calf possesses a smooth surface and is used for elegant shoes, while Scotch-grain cowhide is favored for more casual shoes.

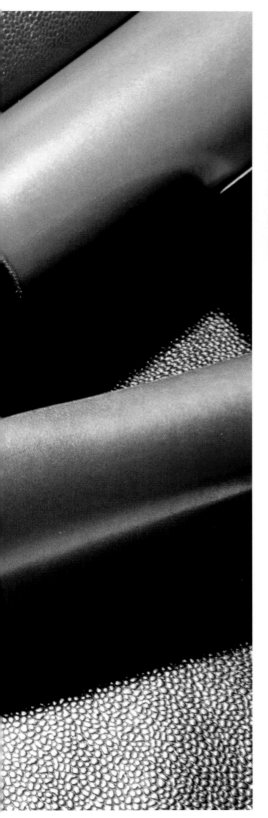

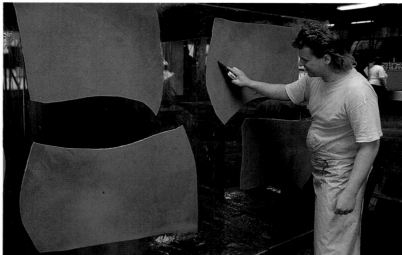

"Striking out" the leather on a glass plate ensures a perfect surface

Post-tanning Procedures and Finishing

There are a number of procedures carried out after tanning and before the final finishing of the leather. After pressing out the excess water, the tanner checks the leather yet again for any defects that may be present. Now the leather is colored to precise specifications. Generally, this is done by one of two procedures: dyeing or staining. In dyeing, the skins are placed into huge tubs and rotated in organic or inorganic dye until it has penetrated all the fibers; in staining, the tanner simply applies the dye onto the surface of the leather. This used to be done with a brush, but today spray guns are more common for this procedure.

The dyed skins can also be dried by several methods. In convection drying, the skins and hides are hung up and conveyed through a drying tunnel 66 feet [20 m] long. "Striking out," a more traditional method, involves placing the leather grain-side down on a large glass plate and pushing a blunt blade across it to remove any moisture and creases there may be in the material. The oldest, but still the most practical, method involves stretching the leather on wooden frames. In both cases, whether it is spread out on a glass plate or a wooden frame, the leather dries at a temperature of 100–140°F [40-60°C] and is left to rest for one or two days. After this the tanner treats the surface of the leather with fats in order to improve its softness and shine. The last stage in the tanning process is smoothing. The fleshside is ironed with a heavy hand-held iron or the leather flattened ("plated") in a machine in which a rolling cylinder presses the grain side of the leather onto a steel sheet heated to 180-190°F [80-90°C]. The chrome-tanned upper leather is now finished and ready to go to the shoemaker's workshop.

Clicking

Before shoemaking became industrialized, the shoemaker cut out every single piece of the shoe himself. Today he is only responsible for the components required to actually build the shoe, such as the sole, the insole, and the welt. The upper leather selected at the tannery - box calf, cowhide, or horse leather - is sent together with the designer's patterns to expert "clickers," who cut out the individual pieces from the leather with knives. Of course, a good clicker must be familiar with the whole process of shoe manufacture and the various properties of the different leathers available.

"We have a great deal of responsibility," says György Szkala, who has been working as a clicker for more than 30 years (and is currently employed at the workshop of L. Vass in Budapest), "because top-quality box calf is a very expensive material. If we do not work carefully enough we cut rejects or waste instead of correctly sized and shaped vamps and quarters. Even the best finished leather has some parts that are more valuable and some that are less valuable. We therefore have to know whether we are supposed to cut the different components of the shoe upper out of the good leather near the spine, or the less precious neck and belly leather. Experience is the best guide, but every piece of box calf is different. That is why the arrangement of the patterns always has to be given careful thought each time.

"If it turns out later that a vamp cut from the most valuable part of the box calf has a defect in it, we use that piece for a smaller part of the shoe. If the knife accidentally slips when we are cutting a part out and it ends up smaller than the carefully designed pattern, it will find a use elsewhere.

"The direction of stretch of a piece of leather is also important. For example, the pattern for the vamp must be laid onto the leather in such a way that the piece cut out can stretch lengthwise, but not sideways. By contrast, the quarter must not stretch lengthwise because otherwise it may become about a half inch [1-2 cm] longer after being worn for a while and destroy the shoe's rigidity and shape.

"In comparison to this, clicking itself is child's play: as long as the knife is sharp enough and you have a steady hand, you can't go wrong."

A good clicker makes a massive contribution to the beauty and durability of the shoe by selecting the leather and cutting out the parts of the shoe upper. The clicker is the expert when it comes to the various colors, the weight, the grain, and the flexibility of different leathers.

First of all, each piece of leather is scrutinized very closely by the clicker to see if there are any defects in it overlooked during the checks at the tannery, such as fleshing cuts, insect bites, or creases. The defects are then marked with a pencil so that these parts of the leather are not on any account used for the upper parts and can be avoided when laying on the patterns.

The clicker pulls the leather in all directions in order to determine its direction of stretch and find out how elastic it is. The patterns are always laid on the leather in the same, strict order: the most important part of the shoe is always the vamp, which is laid on first, then followed by the quarters and, finally, the other components. The vamps are cut out of one or two bands of leather next to the spine. The other pieces to be cut come from less valuable parts of the skin.

The clicker uses the same cutting technique, regardless of which leather the upper is being made of - box calf, cowhide, or cordovan (horse leather). The leather is laid out on a cutting table covered with a sheet of rubber about 3 inches [8 cm] thick. The clicker can cut into the rubber without leaving traces because it just closes up again. The individual parts of the left and right shoes must always be cut in pairs so that they come from the same piece of leather and have the same qualities. The clicker counts the parts and arranges them economically on the skin or hide: two vamps, four quarters, two back straps, four eyelet linings, and, where the design is more complicated, additional single parts. The distance between two parts is often as little as a twenty-fifth of an inch [1 mm].

Finally, the clicker presses the patterns onto the leather and cuts out the vamps, the quarters, and the other parts of the upper. The knife looks very much like a scalpel. The clicker keeps sharpening it with a whetstone so that it does not slip and cause mistakes as he cuts the leather. If the knife is blunt, the cut edges may be jagged or wavy, which would make the closer's work considerably more difficult to carry out.

The name of the customer or an identification number is written on each of the parts once it has been cut out to identify exactly which pair of shoes it belongs to and whether it is part of a right, or left, shoe. Lastly, the parts are tied together, placed in a small bag, and sent to the closer for the upper to be assembled in the traditional expert fashion.

The two-part vamp patterns for a shoe with a winged toe cap are laid onto a piece of box calf.

The clicker's most important tools are a cutting knife made of flexible steel and a whetstone.

Box Calf

Most high-class footwear is made of box calf. This type of calfskin is given heavily grained and smooth finishes. There are three explanations for the term "box calf": the first is that it is derived from the emblem of a leading American leather manufacturer, which showed a calf in a box; the second is based on the fact that the perfectly prepared calfskins were stored and transported in boxes in order to stop them from deteriorating; the third explanation derives the term from the London shoemaker Joseph Box, after whom the leather is supposedly named. Box calf feels soft, but keeps its shape and is highly prized among the different leather varieties. Its grain side has an extraordinarily fine grain with a beautiful pattern. Box calf is about a twenty-fifth of an inch [between 1 and 1.2 mm] thick, and an average skin measures 10.8-16.2 square feet [1-1.5m²] (leather is measured in feet on the international market, but we have given metric measurements as well for readers familiar with the metric system). If only a small number of parts are needed when making the upper of a shoe, as is the case with the Derby, which has an undivided vamp, up to three pairs of shoe uppers can be made from one piece of box calf. There are a number of different ways in which this could be done, but the true craftsmen in the shoemakers' workshop are well practiced in selecting the optimum arrangement for the cutting.

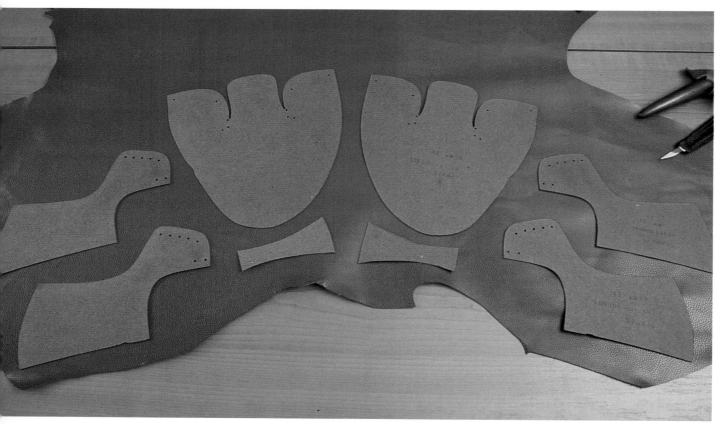

The upper of a Derby consists of an undivided vamp, two quarters, and a back strap. When the skin is laid out the spine runs along the center line from the neck to the rear of the belly. The vamp patterns are arranged symmetrically down the middle of the skin: the right vamp to the right of the spine and the left vamp to its left. As several shoe uppers can be cut from one piece of calfskin, the patterns are laid one after the other down the spine in one or two rows. Vamps cannot be cut from the neck because the structure of the leather there is much looser and there are occasional neck folds, which would detract from the firm, elegant appearance of the vamp. The quarters and back straps are cut from the remaining leather.

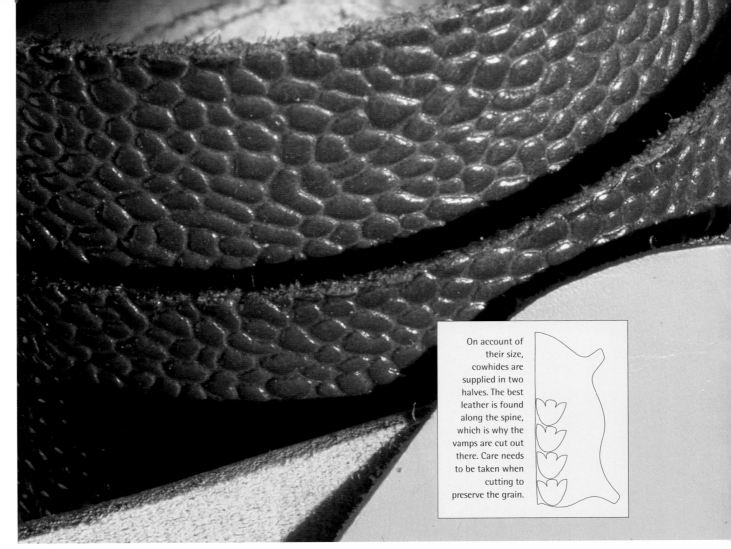

On account of their size, cowhides are supplied in two halves. The best leather is found along the spine, which is why the vamps are cut out there. Care needs to be taken when cutting to preserve the grain.

Grained cowhide has usually been finished with an artificial grain layer.

Cowhide

Cowhide is a material used for heavy working shoes. Its structure is dense, and the fibers of its flesh layer are stronger than those of box calf, but it is flexible (see also page 130). A cowhide must be tough enough to withstand at least 20,000 flexes during its working life without the leather tearing or becoming fragile. Its original surface is seldom visible because it is usually treated and covered with a man-made grain layer - uneven Scotch grain, for example, which has a pleasing appearance.

Cowhides are several times larger than box calf skins, measuring up to 30 square feet [3 m²]. As a result, cowhides are often cut in two along the spine and delivered to the clickers in two halves. The clicker follows a different principle when laying out the patterns of the upper parts on the leather than when cutting box calf. Again, the leather along the spine is the most valuable, but as a tanned cowhide has always been halved down the middle, the clicker lays the vamps of the right and left shoes not opposite each other across the spine, but one after another along the spine. The direction of stretch is a crucial consideration when working with leather that has an artificial grain. If the leather stretches too much, the uneven surface will flatten out when the shoes are worn, and the character of the grain will be lost. It is this very surface that makes a Scotch-grain shoe so individual, attractive, and interesting. This is one more challenge for the expert clicker, who will have spent many years learning his trade.

A number of concealed reinforcements inside the shoe increase the durability of this box-calf Derby upper.

The closer reinforces the thin box calf of this Derby toe cap by gluing in strips of cloth.

Cordovan

Originally, "cordovan" meant a very light goatskin from the Spanish city of Córdoba treated with special tanning materials. The term now refers mainly to a durable form of horse leather. It is perfectly suited for uppers of classic shoes with robust lines. Due to the material's durability, cordovan shoes are usually made with a built-up sole and thicker lining than usual. Probably the most tasteful style for a cordovan shoe is the Budapest.

Shoes made of cordovan leather are hardly any heavier than box-calf shoes. Since a box-calf shoe weighs about 1 pound [500 g] and a cordovan shoe about 19 ounces [540-550 g], the difference between a pair of cordovan shoes and a pair of box-calf shoes will be 2 ounces [80-100 g] at most. Cordovan leather is one of the most expensive materials for shoe uppers, partly due to its outstanding qualities, partly because only two small ovals or circles of leather measuring approx. 30 square feet [3 m²] from the rear, or croup, of this relatively large animal can be used for shoe uppers. It is therefore true to say that one horse equals one pair of shoes.

Cordovan is about a half inch [1.6-1.8 mm] thick, but it is just as soft as box calf. When laying the patterns onto cordovan, the clicker has no fixed points to guide him, such as the spine on box calf or cowhide. He must test the leather with his hands to find out which areas of the hide are dense and which have a looser structure, and lay on the patterns in such a way that the matching parts of the two shoes are of the same thickness. While the shafts through which the hair roots run, the follicles, are completely invisible on box calf, not all traces can be rubbed off or removed when cordovan is finished. These pores are closed up by the application of a special cream and polished to create a shiny surface as smooth as a mirror.

The cordovan leather from one horse is sufficient for a single pair of Budapest shoes.

Exotic Leathers

Lizard skin

When it is stretched out, a lizard leather measures about 10 square feet [1 m²]. This means that at least three or four lizard skins are needed for one pair of shoes. Cutting the parts for an upper out of lizard skin is a real test of the clicker's skills. It is impossible to cut two vamps from one piece of lizard skin, so two skins are needed of approximately the same color and patterning. The vamps are cut out where the leather is thickest and the scale pattern is most attractive. Symmetry can only be achieved if it is possible to find a symmetrical axis running through both skins.

Particularly beautiful lizard-skin shoes are made by assembling the uppers out of many small components. Combinations of lizard leather and smooth box calf are also extraordinarily attractive.

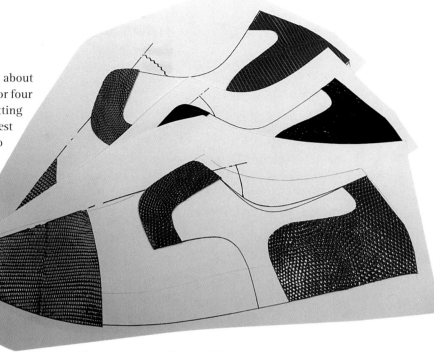

The vamp, counter, and facings of this shoe are made of lizard leather.

Crocodile skin

The skin of baby crocodiles is best suited for the manufacture of shoe uppers from crocodile leather. Once the crocodile has reached a certain size, the scales grow too large and strong, and break easily when the leather is worked. The upper parts for one pair of shoes can be cut from one crocodile skin. When the clicker lays the patterns on the leather he must make sure that the pattern of scales is similar on both shoes.

The direction of stretch is not of much concern when cutting either lizard skin or crocodile skin. As these leathers are much thinner and make more noise than box calf, for example, an interlining is used to support the upper. Saurian leather is often fixed onto an interlining of thin box calf, which must have a degree of elasticity. Shoes of saurian leather are not decorated or stitched. Nor do they have patterns of holes punched in them, because the material is magnificent and rare enough on its own without additional decorations. The effect of crocodile skin can be artificially created with other leathers.

The patterns of scales on lizard leather (left) and crocodile leather (right) are all the decoration that exclusive shoes need.

A number of concealed reinforcements inside the shoe increase the durability of this box-calf Derby upper.

The closer reinforces the thin box calf of this Derby toe cap by gluing in strips of cloth.

Accessories for Shoe Uppers

The uppers of hand-sewn bespoke shoes are always lined. Apart from covering the reinforcements and stiffeners, this also makes the shoes much more comfortable to wear. The upper parts may be made of soft, though durable leather, but when the shoes are made they are treated in many ways as the soft leather is given a final, lasting form. Not only is the upper leather built up and strengthened during the tanning process, various reinforcements are also added as the shoe is made. The lining covers these reinforcements, which would otherwise rub the wearer's feet.

Unlike upper leather, the leather used for linings is not chrome tanned but vegetable tanned. This ensures that the skin of the wearer's feet can breathe naturally. Calfskin is the best material for linings. Its air and moisture permeability are outstanding, and it is elastic, pleasantly soft, and extraordinarily hard-wearing.

The patterns used to cut the parts of the upper and the lining are quite different. It is most important that the seams of the upper and the lining are not placed in direct proximity to each other because then they would tend to press and chafe the foot. The lining should also be made of as few parts as possible in order to reduce the number of seams inside the shoe. This is the reason why the patterns that the clicker uses to cut out the parts of the lining are drawn separately.

The other accessories, some of which are also cut from the same leather as the upper, include various backings and stiffeners. For example, when making a full-brogue shoe, backings are glued in under the decorative brogueing on the toe cap, the quarters, the top line of the quarters, and even the upper edge of the tongue. One refined, decorative way of reinforcing cut edges is the addition of a collar (see page 111), which is also made from the same leather as the upper.

Often the clicker inserts additional strips of cloth to reinforce the vamp and the quarters, particularly when shoes are intended to be particularly firm in their shape. This could be more important with shoes made of softer leather, particulary so if the wearer expects to put them on for more formal occasions, when a casual appearance would not be acceptable.

Apart from the vamp and the quarters, various accessories are cut out of the same leather, such as facing linings and collars.

The color of the leather shows that this is a lining being cut.

Preparations for Assembling the Shoe Upper

The closer marks the seams . . .

The cut edges are hardened by singeing.

. . . and the eyelets.

The cut edges are stained.

The edges that are to be sewn together are skived.

The quarters are ready for further work.

Once the upper, the lining, and the accessories have been cut out, they go from the clickers to the closers. In earlier shoemaker's workshops, making uppers, or "closing," was one of a series of different tasks performed by a single shoemaker. Today, however, closing is a completely separate profession.

A sewing machine is used to stitch the uppers together. This requires some preparation. First of all, the closer marks the edges where the parts of the upper will be joined together. Then he marks in where the decorations and the eyelets will be cut and punched.

An important part of the preparations is the job of paring down the edges that will be stitched together. This is known as "skiving." If the edges were not skived, the double thickness of leather at the seams would cause a ridge to form. However, where skived edges meet, the join is made perfect.

Of course, there are parts of the upper with edges that never come into contact with any other part, such as the top line of the quarters and the upper edge of the tongue. In other places, two pieces of leather overlap in such a way that the upper edge is strongly emphasized, for example on straight or winged toe caps. Who would have imagined the care and painstaking work devoted to giving these edges an attractive appearance? The methods that have been developed to this end vary considerably in their sophistication. One of the less complicated techniques involves turning the cut edge over and simply sewing the folded material down. More refined techniques include gimping and the addition of a collar (see pages 105 and 111).

Before an edge is turned over, gimped, or reinforced with a collar, the closer skives the cut edges of the upper and singes them in order to harden the edges and remove any tiny remnants of leather left after cutting. When a piece of leather has been stained, the material is lighter on the inside. For this reason a sponge soaked in dye is wiped around the cut edges in order to create uniformity of color, and to give the finished item a professionalism befitting the craft.

Gimping

Gimping serves not only to remove weak cut edges, but also has a decorative function. This technique is most effective when it is applied to the uppers of shoes that are assembled from more than the average number of components, because it helps to create varied patterns that match the complexity of a more elaborate construction. Often the upper edge of the tongue, or even the whole tongue, is gimped as well, in order to create a harmonious and pleasing effect.

The gimping machine functions on the same principle as the sewing machine, but, instead of needles, it is fitted with steel tools of varying sizes, designs, and shapes. The closer uses these tools to cut straight, or curved, serrated patterns along the edges. After the gimping has been completed, these edges are also stained with a sponge so that the colors match.

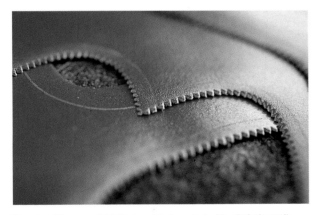

The winged toe cap of this Budapest is decorated with relatively small, regular serrated patterns.

Gimping decorates and strengthens cut edges. The gimped edges of the quarters can also be reinforced with a collar.

The closer uses a gimping machine to cut serrated patterns along the cut edges, creating distinctive decorative effects.

Brogueing

All the classic men's shoes can be purchased in a smooth version without any brogueing and a brogued version with holes punched in it (see also the chapter on Shoe Styles). A semi-brogue (also known as a half-brogue) is a shoe on which the seams on the upper are decorated with brogueing and there is a straight toe cap at the most noticeable part of the foot, the front. A full brogue is a shoe with brogueing on its winged toe cap as well as its seams. The brogueing along the seams runs in rows and sequences. Where brogueing is added to the toe cap or, less often, the quarters, it is arranged in artistic, geometrical patterns of various sizes.

The brogueing along the seams emphasizes the lines and curves where the parts of the upper join. It is placed on the seams between the vamp and the quarters, the counter and the quarters, and where there is a straight, or winged, toe cap the toe cap and the apron. The top line of the quarters can also be decorated with rows of brogueing to great effect.

The simplest arrangement of brogueing along the seams is one in which holes an eighth of an inch [3 mm] in diameter are punched at intervals of a quarter of an inch [5 mm]. A more complicated version has small and large holes alternating. Two holes a third of the size are punched in each of the gaps between the larger holes.

In general, brogueing is punched at some distance from the edge of the leather. This makes it possible to sew one or more seams along it on both sides.

No pattern is made for the perforations along the seams and the intervals between the holes are not marked. The closer relies on a good eye and an intuitive feel developed by years of experience. He spreads out the part on a rubber block, places the sharp-edged punch vertically onto the leather, strikes it crisply with a hammer, and punches hole after hole in a steady rhythm.

In this way, the closer ensures that the brogued shoe presents a pleasing appearance, casual but smart. The brogue was popularized by the Prince of Wales in the 1930s, and his sense of style continues to be copied today by many gentlemen.

A sharp-edged punch with a diameter of a twentieth, an eighth, or a quarter inch [1, 3, or 5 mm] is used to punch brogueing.

A perfect row of brogueing is created as the closer punches the leather in a steady rhythm.

First, holes an eighth of an inch [3 mm] in diameter are punched at regular intervals along the seams on the quarters.

Two smaller parallel holes are then added in each of the gaps between the large holes.

The curve of this winged tip is decorated with holes of various sizes in alternating sequences, in pairs and singly.

Decorations on the Toe Cap

The toe cap at the front of a semi-brogue or full-brogue shoe is decorated with artistic geometric brogueing. Holes of varying or equal sizes are arranged in extraordinarily varied geometrical shapes and patterns. The lines of these patterns may be straight or curved, but they are always symmetrical. Most decorations are patterns of alternating holes an eighth and a twenty-fifth of an inch [3 and 1 mm] across, though sometimes an even larger hole (a quarter inch [5 mm] across) is placed in the center of the brogueing. However, the decorative pattern should never take over the whole tip of the shoe. The customer can choose from among the patterns held by the shoe designer, but it is also possible for a new, and therefore individual, decorative pattern to be designed exclusively for his shoes if he makes a special request.

From a technical point of view, the perforations on the tip of the shoe are made in exactly the same way as the brogueing along the seams, except that here the closer uses a pattern drawn up by the shoe designer. He places a thin piece of paper with the pattern on it over the leather and carefully uses the punch to stamp perforations in the leather at the points indicated by the designer.

As the sequences of brogueing are punched along the joins between the various components of the upper, for example along the joins between the quarters and the vamp, the leather of the lower part will inevitably be visible under the holes. When there is brogueing on the toe cap of the shoe, either the toe puff, which is used to give shape to the toe, or, if the shoe is made without a toe puff, the leather of the lining shows through the holes. In order to avoid this color clash, a thin backing made of the same material as the upper is glued in under these perforations.

Brogueing may be added to a shoe for more than just esthetic reasons. It can also be extremely practical. Brogueing makes many summer shoes cool, allowing air to circulate freely round the wearer's feet.

Large holes are surrounded by circles and straight lines of small holes.

A characteristic arabesque dominated by curving lines.

The closer follows a pattern as he punches the decorations on the toe cap.

Holes of differing sizes give this strict geometric arrangement a more relaxed feel.

Perfect harmony is created here between the brogueing along the seams and the decorative pattern on the toe cap.

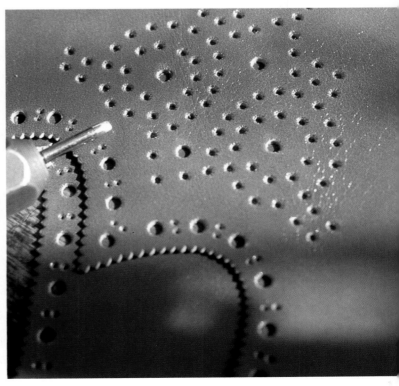

The closer reinforces the vamp and the quarters with leather, or textile, backings.

A leather backing with skived edges all round is laid under the eyelets.

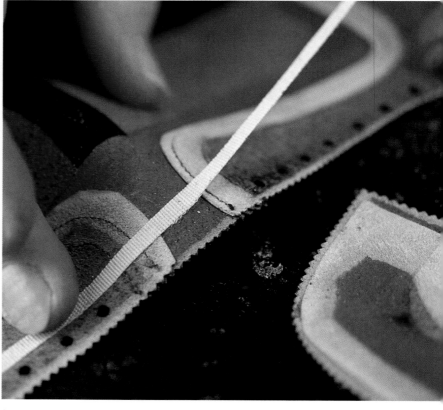

Slots are cut in the collar where it bends sharply to stop it becoming too tight or bunching up.

A strong textile tape prevents the stitched quarters from stretching out of shape.

Reinforcing the Upper

As discussed above, various reinforcements are added to the upper. They ensure that the shape formed during shoemaking does not change but remains stable and elegant for years on end. Some of these reinforcements are inserted by the closer, others are added by the shoemaker himself at later, more crucial, stages of the shoemaking process.

The most important consideration is to reinforce those points at which the danger of stretching is the greatest, along the top line of the quarters, for example. A band of fabric an eighth to a quarter inch [3-5 mm] wide is added here for this purpose. This band must be strong enough not to tear, but not completely inelastic. The closer also inserts cloth of roughly the same thickness as a bed sheet between the upper and the lining of the quarters and the vamp.

These reinforcements are glued into the upper with an adhesive solution of rubber dissolved in benzine. This adhesive dries within 10-15 minutes and remains flexible and elastic even once it has dried.

The closer reinforces any parts that might be easily damaged when the shoe is worn, such as the toe of the shoe, with backings and stiffeners made of the same leather as the upper. Another sensitive area is the leather around the eyelets, where the facing rips easily if the wearer pulls his laces too tight. For this reason this part of the upper is reinforced with particular care. The closer glues lining strips about three-quarters to an inch [2-2.5 cm] wide under the upper, punches the eyelets through both layers of leather, and then stitches the lining to the edge of the quarter.

The tape glued and stitched to the quarters prevents the leather from stretching, but will not necessarily stop the cut edge along the top line of the quarter from tearing. A special form of reinforcement is used to strengthen this edge: the collar. A strip of leather about three-quarters of an inch [1.8 cm] wide is cut and its edges skived. It is folded in half lengthwise and stitched together to make a double-strength band. This is glued to the cut edges, and later stitched on as well. About a twentieth of an inch [1-1.5 mm] of the collar can be seen above the cut edges, any more would not be esthetically pleasing.

The collar is glued onto the top line of the quarter.

The color of the top thread should be one tone darker than the leather.

The color of the bottom thread must match that of the top thread.

The seams of the upper must always be stitched accurately and evenly.

Stitching the Upper

The earliest humans (approx. 50,000 BC) sewed the pieces of leather they used as clothing together with thorns, fish and animal bones, and tendons. The first real sewing needles have been found by archeologists excavating sites that date from the Bronze Age (3000-1000 BC). They were thin pieces of bronze with holes drilled in them through which the thread was pulled. Needles of exactly the same design were used to stitch all shoe uppers until the middle of the nineteenth century. They are often still used today when making uppers and soles.

In 1845 the American inventor Elias Howe (1819-1867), who worked as a machinist in a textile mill, built the first practical sewing machine capable of producing lock stitch. The designers of the modern stitching machines have perfected the principles upon which this historic machine functioned.

The arrangement of stitching on the upper is determined by two main considerations: the seams must be strong and durable, and they must run in straight, regular lines. In addition, they should also be esthetically pleasing.

Several seams may be sewn parallel to each other. It is usually enough to have a single or double seam along the top line of the quarter. However, where the upper is placed under greater stress, as, for example, where the vamp and the quarters join, four seams are often sewn next to each other. In a delicate operation, the seams are sewn about a twentieth of an inch apart with five or six stitches to a half inch [1cm].

As a rule, cotton thread is used to stitch the thin parts of the upper, stronger linen thread for the thick leather. Silk thread is recommended for stitching very fine parts of the upper. The thread used to stitch shoe uppers consists of three, four, six, or nine strands. The fineness of the thread is calculated from the relationship between its length (measured in meters) and its weight (measured in grams). Thus, the figure 80/4 on a roll of thread means that 80 m of thread weighs 4 g. When a lock-stitch seam is sewn on a machine, a top and bottom thread loop round each other and so "lock" several layers of material together. The top thread is visible on the outside of the upper, the bottom thread runs along the inside of the shoe.

Seams often function as decorations. Interesting effects can be created when the closer works with varying thread weights and stitch sizes. For example, it is possible to emphasize the casual styling of a shoe by using thick thread and large stitches (three stitches to a half inch [1 cm]), or expertly combining narrow and thick seams next to each other.

Before the closer can begin stitching the seams, he marks all the edges that are to be fixed together, applies a rubber solution, and glues them together as marked. This makes sewing the shoe much easier because it stops the parts slipping while they are being stitched. The seams must always run accurately and evenly. Any irregularity would destroy the harmony of a superb piece of footwear, but closers are well regarded for their craftsmanship and there is rarely any danger of their work not being up to scratch.

The apron and toe cap are stitched together.

The closer fixes the vamp onto the quarter.

The counter and quarter are glued and then stitched together.

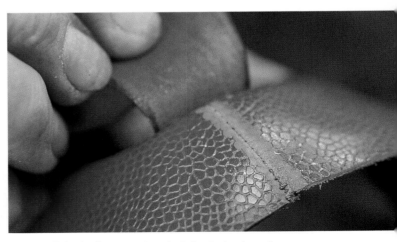

If the shoe has no counter, a back strap is placed over the seam.

The Lining

Although different patterns are used when the upper and the lining are cut out and the two are assembled separately, they fit together perfectly. They are stitched to each other along the top line of the quarters, and nowhere else, because a number of additional reinforcements are added later between the two layers, such as the toe puff, the side supports, and the counter.

The lining is made up of three parts - the vamp and two quarters. It is pleasantly soft yet hard-wearing, and is fitted into the shoe upper with its grain side facing into the shoe. However, a special trick is used when lining slippers. The lining of a slipper consists of four parts - the vamp, two short quarters, and a separate piece of leather that joins the two quarters at the heel. When the lining is assembled, this heel section is inserted the other way round so that the matt flesh side faces into the shoe inner. It is more adhesive than the grain side and it stops the wearer's foot from slipping out of the shoe.

Men's Derby and Oxford shoes are lined in different ways. The tongue of the Derby is lined together with the vamp, since both are cut out of a single piece of leather. However, as the tongue on an Oxford shoe is a separate piece of leather, it is lined first of all and then stitched onto the vamp.

Summer shoes are not lined because uppers decorated with brogueing or woven leather ensure the air permeability of the shoe. Nevertheless, summer shoes and sandals are often given a thin inner lining in order to help them keep their shape. On shoes with brogueing punched in them, the closer punches the upper leather together with the leather lining. Sandals are given a full lining, which is stitched to the straps. The superfluous sections between the straps are then carefully cut out with a sharp knife.

The upper and the lining are stitched together at the edge of the quarter.

The lining is fitted into a Derby shoe.

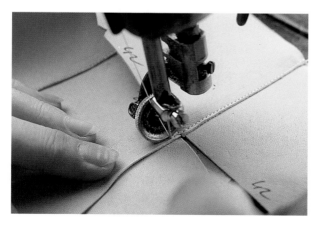

Both quarters are lined with leather.

Finishing the Upper

Even when the upper has been carefully stitched and lined, there is still work to be done before it can go on to the shoemaker. First, the leather lining is trimmed along the top line of the quarters, about a twenty-fifth of an inch [1-2 mm] above the seam. The cut edge must be absolutely straight, so that the leather of the lining does not show above the top line of the quarter, and the shears must not damage the seam.

After this, the eyelets are punched out. Mostly, they have a diameter of about an eighth of an inch [2-3 mm] and are placed at intervals of a half to three-quarters of an inch [1-1.5 cm]. The eyelets should be small, so that it is initially rather difficult to pull the shoe laces through them because, as time passes, the holes stretch when the laces are tied.

After each piece of stitching is finished, the remaining thread is cut off except for a small loose end, which is cut down very short by the closer. These loose ends are dealt with by drawing the top thread through the upper and lining to the inside of the shoe with a sharp awl and knotting it firmly to the end of the bottom thread. Any remaining pieces of thread are cut off or burnt away.

As the upper still has to go through plenty of testing treatment during the construction of the shoe, there is no need to worry about cleaning and polishing at this stage. However, if the shoe is a full-brogue, the closer has one more job to do: a leather backing is stuck under the perforated toe cap with a rubber solution so that no dust or leather particles get into the decorations during the subsequent work. Traces of adhesive are removed from the larger holes with a piece of rubber, and the upper is now ready for delivery to the shoemaker.

The lining must be carefully trimmed.

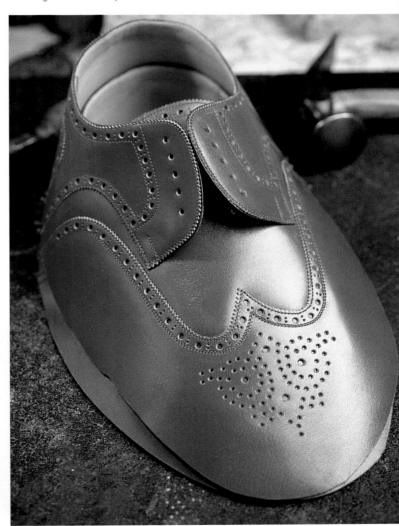
The upper of a full-brogue Budapest ready for delivery to the shoemaker.

Punching the eyelets.

The Shoe

The Shoemaker's Workshop

The shoemaking profession began about 15,000 years ago, when people first made protective coverings for their feet. During the Stone Age, the women of the family were responsible for making shoes. When separate clans joined to form larger communities, a division of labor soon developed and, as with other crafts, the task of making shoes would be assigned to one member of the group.

What must be one of the earliest depictions of the shoemaker's trade appears on an Egyptian wall painting in the tomb of Rekhmire in Thebes, illustrating a number of different crafts in a kind of strip-cartoon style; shipbuilders, jewelers, sculptors, and scribes are featured along with shoemakers. The well-equipped workshop where they are making sandals shows that at this time shoemakers already occupied a respected position among the various trades, and consequently were honored by a place on a wall painting in the burial chamber of the vizier who served Thutmosis III.

This ancient Egyptian sandal workshop practiced division of labor: the operation involved in stretching the leather was already clearly distinct from the process of punching holes in the sole through which straps could be pulled later.

The painting on this Greek amphora of the sixth century BC (British Museum, London) shows a shoemaker cutting out his leather. There are tools and models for shoes above his head. The Greek shoemaker works at a horizontal bench, where his customer is trying on shoes.

The cobbler on this tombstone relief from Reims, France (*circa* second century AD) is working on a shoe stretched on a stand. There is a basket full of leather patches at his feet, and his tools hang on the wall.

According to a tradition of classical antiquity the second king of Rome, Numa Pompilius (715–672 BC), wishing to avoid endless disputes between Roman citizens, classified them all by their origins into nine associations (Lat. *collegia*). The shoemakers (Lat. *sutores*) were the fifth *collegium*. However, there is no historical evidence for the existence of craft unions similar to guilds until the second century BC, during the period of the Roman Republic. These associations were state controlled, and their main task was to regulate communal worship and social occasions, and look after the joint professional interests of their members. Individual craftsmen lived closer together, setting up workshops in close proximity to each other in the side streets of large town centers. Shoemakers used to live and work in streets with names like "Shoe Lane" and "Shoemakers' Alley," which still survive today in many towns and cities.

Documentary evidence for the existence of the craft of shoemaking in the German-speaking countries dates only from the end of the sixth century AD in Burgundian law, and in the ninth century in the laws of Charlemagne (Capitulary XLV, on feudal estates), in which the estate administrators are instructed to seek out good craftsmen ". . . such as blacksmiths, gold and silversmiths, cobblers, turners . . .".

The period around the tenth and eleventh centuries brought the first major change in the history of shoemaking: shoemakers joined together in guilds which from then on represented their economic and social interests. Those of them who moved away from the country and into towns enjoyed not only the protection of the guilds but also the economic advantages of markets and trading centers. At first the guilds were subject to episcopal law, and as a result the clergy tended to be a dominant influence on their social life.

The patron saints of medieval shoemakers were the brothers Crispinus and Crispinianus, whose festival is still celebrated on 25 October. According to a French legend they were brothers of noble Roman birth (Crépin and Crépinien in French, Crispin and Crispinian in English) who converted to Christianity, and fled from Rome during the persecutions of the Emperor Diocletian (AD 284–305), taking refuge in Soissons. They learned the shoemaking trade, preached the gospel by day, and by night made shoes which they gave away to the poor. Their virtuous conduct made them many enemies, and in the end they were betrayed to the Roman commander Maximianus Herculius. But torture could not harm them – legend says that the iron spikes driven into their fingertips sprang out again, injuring a number of bystanders instead – and nor could the millstones hung around their necks in an attempt to drown them. Finally, the brothers were beheaded. The soldiers threw their bodies to the wild beasts, but the animals refused to touch them. According to another tradition, an old man and his sister were told by angels to bury the corpses near Soissons; in yet another version their fellow believers buried them in the church of St Laurence in Panisperma, Italy. The citizens of Soissons (the seat of a Catholic bishop from the third century AD) dedicated a church to the saints, and the relics of the holy brothers were finally laid to rest in Osnabrück in the ninth century.

An English tradition says that the brothers were sons of the queen of Kent. Persecuted by the Roman commander Maximianus Herculius, they fled to Faversham in Kent, disguised as poor peasants. Crispin apprenticed himself to a shoemaker, while Crispinian joined the Roman army. One day Crispin's master sent him to deliver a new pair of shoes to the daughter of the Imperator Maximianus (whom Diocletian appointed co-regent with him in AD 288). Ursula and Crispin fell in love and married secretly. When Maximianus heard the news, he was mollified by the brothers' noble birth and the heroic deeds done by Crispinian in the Roman army, and he gave official recognition to the couple's marriage on 25 October.

It does not matter which story you prefer – or how much truth there is in either of them – the two saints are now firmly established as the shoemaking trade's patron saints. Their devotion to the craft must be an inspiration to many master shoemakers and, perhaps more so, to those just beginning to learn the art of shoemaking.

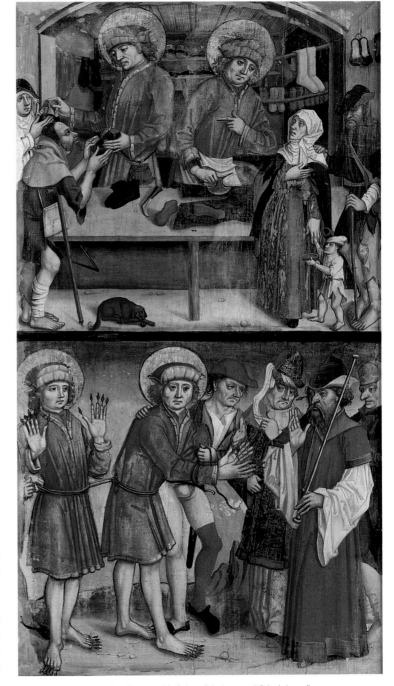

Above, the altarpiece "Two Scenes with Saints Crispinus and Crispinianus" by the Bernese Master of the Pinks (1500–1510) shows the brothers giving away their shoes to the poor. Below, the two saints are being led away after torture to their execution (Schweizerisches Landesmuseum, Zurich).

The Shoemakers' Guilds

Medieval craft guilds developed at the end of the eleventh century. In Germany, according to documents that have come down to us, a shoemakers' guild was founded in 1104 in Trier. Others followed: guilds were founded in Würzburg in 1128, in Bremen in 1274, and in Frankfurt am Main in 1377. A document recording the founding of the Guild of Cordwainers in London dates from 1272; the word "cordwainer" for a shoemaker is from the Spanish town of Córdoba, famous for the fine quality of its leather. The guild also contained tanners and curriers (who gave the leather its final treatment), and its motto was *corio et arte*, "with leather and skill." The shoemakers and cobblers of Paris joined together into the Confrérie des Compagnons de Paris in 1379, and there is mention in the records of a guild of shoemakers and cobblers in Zurich in Switzerland at around the same time.

The shoemakers' guilds drew up their own rules and regulations, and ensured that they were strictly observed. They set prices and stipulated high standards of quality control, regulating production as well as working hours, conditions for acceptance into the guild, and the training of apprentices and journeymen. They also organized the social life of their members.

Documents and money were kept in the guild chest, which was entrusted to the safekeeping of the most highly respected members of the guild. It was often made in the shape of a folding altar, and contained the names of guild members, documents, valuable drinking cups, shrouds, and other symbols of community life. In large and prosperous cities the guilds had guildhalls where assemblies and meetings were held. They were also available as accommodation for traveling craft journeymen.

Anyone who wished to learn the shoemaking trade had to fulfill a number of conditions. In Germany, he could become an apprentice only if he was "of good and virtuous family on both his father's and his mother's side," or if he had married a shoemaker's widow. Furthermore, the candidate must have spent 14 days in a shoemaker's workshop, giving evidence of his skill and talents. After producing satisfactory proof of his family origins, coming through the trial period successfully, and paying his apprentice's premium, he would agree a contract with his master, whose task it now was to teach the young man all the skills of the trade and ensure that his moral conduct was impeccable. The average apprenticeship was three years, or four years if the apprentice could not pay a premium. After the agreed period was up, and the apprentice had made his journeyman piece, he set out to spend six to nine years as a traveling journeyman, perfecting and extending his technical expertise in other workshops. (In the course of the seventeenth century, the journeyman's travels were cut to a year and a half, and this period became an established part of the shoemaker's training.) During his travels the journeyman spent at least six weeks in each workshop where he stayed; an official document, and later on a notebook of his travels, recorded both the time he had spent in any place and his behavior there. When the shoemaker's journeyman had completed his travels he proceeded to make his masterpiece, displaying his knowledge and skill to four examiners drawn from among the senior guild members. He had to make four pairs

This engraving of a shoemaker's workshop by Abraham Bosse, dating from around 1650, shows the master as a highly respected figure, wearing rich clothes as he stands at the counter of his workshop.

of shoes and boots within eight days. The 1763 statutes of the Würzburg guild stipulate the following items: "One pair stout riding boots, one fine pair gentlemen's shoes, one pair wooden-heeled women's shoes, one pair wooden-heeled women's clogs." Only after the shoemaker had passed this examination – which was an expensive business for him, since his examiners expected to be lavishly entertained – was he made a master and accepted as a guild member. From now on he and his family were respected in the trade, and enjoyed the economic and social protection of the craft guild to which he now officially belonged.

The records show that shoemakers in towns could lead the life of feudal lords. For instance, in the time of King Henry VIII of England, who died in 1547, a master shoemaker in Fleet Street called John Peachey employed over forty journeymen and apprentices, who even escorted him to church in livery specially designed for them, and carrying swords by their sides. When the master shoemaker John Camps of Cheapside in London died in 1796, he left £37,000 in his will for charitable purposes.

One of the most famous German shoemakers was Hans Sachs (1494–1576), honored not only as a fine master shoemaker but also as an outstanding poet and Meistersinger. He composed over 4000 songs and 85 carnival plays, as well as many realistic and satirical comedies in which he attacked the complacency of the urban craft guilds.

Poorer shoemakers who lived in the country made simple peasants' shoes, strong and inexpensive, for the rural population. Country cobblers, usually working on very dilapidated premises, had a far better reputation than cobblers in towns, and could mend a shoe so well that it looked like new. The traveling cobbler was a countryside character too. He carried the tools of his trade around with him, and made shoes for farmers and their families from their own stocks of leather. Country cobblers represented competition for the urban shoemakers' workshops, and as a result the guilds kept strict watch over the relationship between supply and demand in their home markets. In 1800, for instance, Nuremberg issued a decree forbidding women servants to buy any of their shoes in markets outside that city.

However, local competition was not to be underestimated either. Some workshops employed more journeymen than was permitted, expected their men to work longer hours than the regulation ten hours a day in summer and eleven in winter, or made shoes of models that had not been officially approved. Guild officials checked up on workshops in an attempt to prevent such practices.

The dark earth colors, and the men's serious expressions and bent heads, illustrate the poverty of the cobbler's family in David Ryckaert's oil painting *Cobbler in his Workshop with his Journeymen*, of the year 1684 (Museum der bildenden Künste, Leipzig).

Pictures of craftsmen such as this engraving of *Un Cordonnier*, of around 1750, were very popular during the period of the Enlightenment. Their interest lay chiefly in the practical information they gave about models and manufacturing methods.

It seems that the level of protection provided by the guilds was quite high in an era when workers in other fields could be ruthlessly exploited. Perhaps this was in recognition of the high standards of craftsmanship in the shoemaking profession.

Shoe factories like those owned by the Swiss ribbon and suspender manufacturer C.F. Bally (founded 1851) profited greatly by the technical innovations of the nineteenth century (woodcut, *circa* 1881, Bally Schuhmuseum, Schönenwerd).

Industrialization and its Consequences

After 1750, towns began losing their special political importance. This development, and freedom of trade – a measure introduced in 1791 in France, and at the beginning of the nineteenth century in Prussia and other European states (although it was not finally recognized throughout the whole of Germany until the Trade Law of 1869) – led between them to the dissolution of the old guilds. More modern forms of trade association called *Innungen* developed in the German states, and exist at least in name to this day.

Individual shoemakers fell on hard times with the coming of industrialization in the middle of the nineteenth century. The first functional sewing machine, made by Elias Howe, was followed in 1856 by a machine that could stitch uppers, then in 1860 by the first machine for screwing soles and heels together, and in 1874 by the Goodyear machine that could be used to make welted shoes. Around 1900 McKay's machine for stitching through soles finally brought shoemaking into the machine age. Shoe factories profited enormously by these technical innovations. Textile manufacturing and the shoe trade spread particularly fast in the United States:

by 1901 over a million American shoes had been imported to England. Small shoemaking workshops, unable to compete with the speed of industrial manufacturing or to keep up with falling prices, suffered heavy losses. The shoemaker was downgraded to a mere cobbler who mended shoes. However, the quality factor became the feature distinguishing a factory from a genuine shoemaker's workshop. Many of the workshops that had always set great store by their old traditions found patrons in circles where the belief was (and still is) that shoes as well as clothes make the man, and these customers insisted on individuality and very high quality in their shoes.

In shoemakers' workshops in London, Paris, Rome, Vienna, and Budapest – some of them with a century of past history behind them, but some opened more recently – the ancient traditions of the craft are still preserved. The workshop of László Vass in Budapest, for instance, carefully maintains standards of quality on the old guild principles. Every shoemaker in the Vass workshop proudly acknowledges his own work, loves his job, and enjoys working in a friendly, almost family atmosphere.

Tools and working processes have not changed since 1568, when this woodcut of "The Shoemaker" appeared in a book entitled *Eigentlicher Beschreibung aller Stände auf Erden* ("A True Account of All Ranks of Life on Earth"), by Jost Amman and Hans Sack.

Every shoemaker here in László Vass's workshop is intent on maintaining high standards at every stage of the shoemaking process, and is proud to acknowledge his own handiwork.

Shoemakers in modern Hungary do not have to produce a "masterpiece" such as the guilds used to demand, but every pair of shoes is made with as much care as if it were indeed a masterpiece of that kind; while in Germany a shoemaker's masterpiece still has to pass an examination before he is permitted to open his own workshop and train apprentices.

Shoemakers in traditional workshops use hammer, nails, and cobbler's thread in the same way as their predecessors two thousand years ago. You will see their hands many times in the following pages of this chapter; marked by cuts from knives and thread, shaped by many thousands of hammer blows and stitches, they bear the traces of their past labor. The shoemakers themselves have made most of their own tools. Knives, awls, and needles are the same as those that can be seen in old woodcuts and engravings, and every shoemaker insists almost superstitiously on his own equipment, claiming that anything else does not handle in quite the same way. There is no division of labor in László Vass's workshop; the shoe does not pass from hand to hand, as if on a conveyor belt, with one shoemaker nailing the insole into place, another stitching the welt, and a third perhaps fitting the sole or heel. The whole shoe is made by a single craftsman from beginning to end, and bears the marks of his own method of working. A knowledgeable customer, looking at a finished shoe, can often tell where and by whom it was made.

The shoemaker's bench is a little world in itself. Despite the apparent disorder that reigns, every piece of leather, every thread, the wax, the dye, and all the tools have their own places and their own special functions.

Where the materials and tools are concerned, not much has changed over the centuries. This is very clear if we compare a picture of a sixteenth-century shoemaker's workshop like the one in the 1568 woodcut (above left) with a photograph of one of the modern workshops that still maintain the old traditions. The craftsmen in László Vass's workshop in Budapest are seen working on individual shoes in much the same way as those in the woodcut. The various operations in shoemaking, and even the movements involved, have remained almost identical, as the following pages will amply illustrate.

Construction of the Shoe

The leather for soles and other parts of the lower section of the shoe is placed on the shoemaker's bench, together with the made-to-measure last, identified by name, and the parts of the upper that have been sewn together. Now the shoemaker begins to construct the shoe. "Construction" is an appropriate term, for in the course of his work the shoemaker will fit one part into another, adjusting them over or below each other, thus building the flat surface of the leather of the upper into a three-dimensional shape.

First, using a knife, the shoemaker cuts out the leather for the sections he will need to make the lower part of the shoe – the insole, sole, welt, inside counter, outside counter, inside toe cap, and heel lifts. Work on the upper itself now concludes, and reinforcement sections such as the inside toe cap, the counter, and the side reinforcements are inserted.

The first operation in constructing the shoe is to nail the insole to the last. Working with pliers, the shoemaker then fixes the bottom edge of the upper to the insole.

Stitches set with needle and thread through holes pre-punched at regular intervals fix the welt to the insole as far as the heel area. The first rand, until now the part still missing from the foundation of the shoe, so to speak, is tacked to the heel area with wooden pegs.

A hollow space has now been created between the welt and the outsole, and the shoemaker sets a shank spring inside it. This spring, which has a stabilizing function, is covered with a piece of leather. Cork filling is inserted to occupy the remainder of the hollow space.

For single-soled shoes, the shoemaker now stitches the outsole to the welt; for double-soled shoes, a midsole is placed between the welt and the outsole.

A second rand is now fixed with wooden pegs at the heel area of the sole, and the heel is built up on it. The last has now done its job and can be removed.

The finishing operations give an esthetic touch to the functional form of the shoe. Once it has been scoured and cleaned inside and outside, the leather is polished to a high gloss, ornamentation and regular rows of stitching are emphasized, and the sole acquires a silky sheen.

All tasks we performed with care and attention to detail, to ensure that the final appearance of the shoe truly reflects the shoemaker's art.

The uppers, made-to-measure lasts, records relating to the customer's feet, and leather for the lower parts of the shoe have been delivered to the shoemaker's workshop. Now he has to assemble them into the perfect shoe.

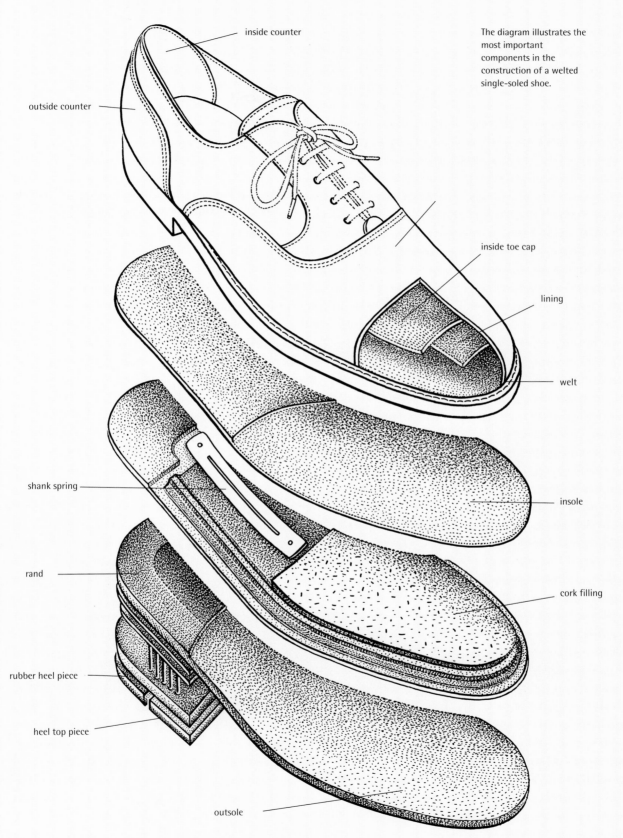

inside counter

outside counter

The diagram illustrates the most important components in the construction of a welted single-soled shoe.

inside toe cap

lining

welt

shank spring

insole

rand

cork filling

rubber heel piece

heel top piece

outsole

The Shoe 125

The ABC of the Shoe

Cork filling

Cork filling in the hollow area created by the fitting of the welt gives the sole a certain springiness and stability as the wearer walks.

Counter

The inside counter is a piece of leather fitted to the place where the two parts of the upper are joined as a reinforcement, and acts as an extension of the heel, holding the foot firmly in the shoe. The outside counter is cut from the leather of the uppers and covers the outside of the stitched sides. It can be either quite a narrow strip or a larger piece of leather matching the shape of the heel.

Heel lifts

The heel is made from two to four pieces of stout leather, known as lifts.

Heel top piece

The outer section of leather on the heel, which comes into direct contact with the ground.

Inside toe cap

A piece of leather one-sixteenth of an inch [1.7–2 mm] thick is cut from the neck area of the hide. Its shape will depend on the model of the shoe, and it is fitted between the leather of the upper and the lining. The inside toe cap gives the toe of the shoe an attractive shape and good support, so that it will not be stretched out of shape by walking or wet weather. It also protects the toes.

Insole

The insole is a piece of leather about one-eighth of an inch [2.5–3.5 mm] thick (depending on the sturdiness of the shoe) on which the shoe is constructed. It is usually covered inside the shoe with a thin leather lining (the insole cover).

Insole cover

This is a soft leather covering fitted over the insole and coming into direct contact with the foot. It may cover the entire length of the insole, three-quarters of it, or only a quarter (under the heel), as the customer wishes.

Lining

The inside of the upper is lined with pit-tanned leather. This lining comes into direct contact with the foot and must therefore be particularly supple and able to "breathe."

Outsole

The part of the shoe that comes into direct contact with the ground. In elegant, lightweight shoes it is about three-sixteenths of an inch [5 mm] thick, and correspondingly thicker in stouter shoes.

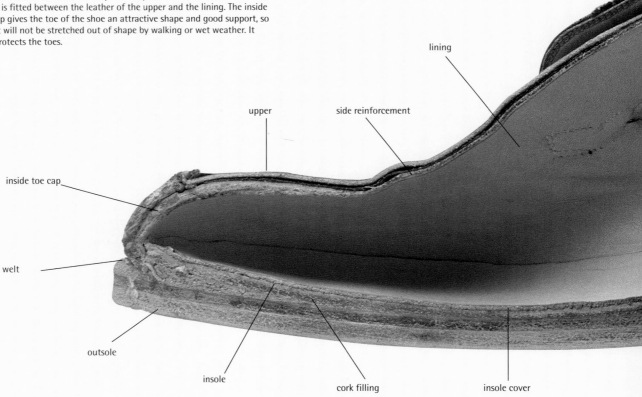

Rand

The rand is a strip of leather three-quarters of an inch [2 cm] wide and one-eighth of an inch [3 mm] thick nailed to the insole and outsole, either supplementing the welt as the basis for the outsole, or forming the foundation of the heel. In welted shoes, the rand is fastened with wooden pegs; in double-stitched shoes it is sewn into place.

Rubber heel piece

A hard, slip-proof rubber piece about a quarter inch [6 mm] thick is fitted to the heel top piece.

Shank spring

The shank spring is a steel spring about 4 inches [10 cm] long and a half inch [1.5 cm] wide, fitted into the hollow space between the welt and the insole, and reaching from about halfway along the heel to the beginning of the ball of the foot (this part of the sole is known as the shank or sometimes the waist). It is shaped to fit the curve of the sole. The shank spring stabilizes the foot as the wearer of the shoe walks, and prevents the heel from wobbling.

Side reinforcements

Side reinforcements are cut from the material of the upper, and fitted to the upper between the outer layer and the leather lining, and between the toe cap and the counter. They are narrow strips of leather that prevent the upper from stretching out of shape, and give good support to both sides of the shoe.

Upper

The shoemaker uses chrome-tanned leather for the uppers.

Welt

This strip of leather, on average 2 feet long, three-quarters of an inch wide, and an eighth of an inch thick [60 cm x 2 cm x 3 mm], is the supporting structure of the shoe. It holds the upper, insole, and sole together.

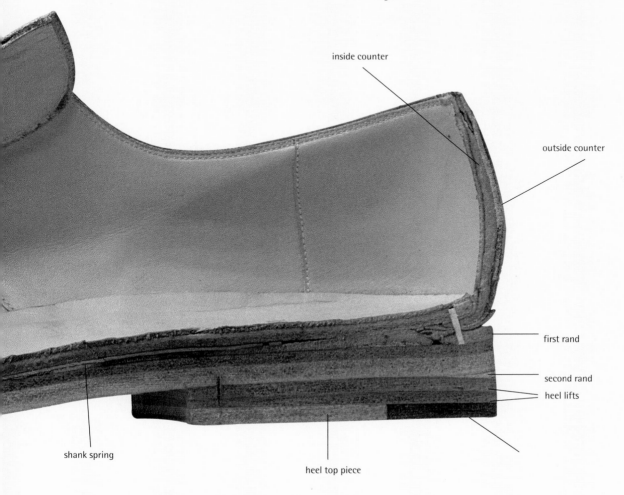

inside counter

outside counter

first rand

second rand

heel lifts

shank spring

heel top piece

The Welted Shoe

Handmade shoes are divided into two types, depending on the way they are made: the welted shoe and the double-stitched shoe.

The basic way in which the upper is fastened to the insole by means of a welt is the same in both types, and so are certain parts of the operation, for instance the technique of stitching with two needles. The following detailed description of the techniques of the making of both types of shoes, however, shows that there are considerable differences between them, whether in respect of their appearance or their function.

The welted shoe, which may have either a single or a double sole, is a lightweight, elegant shoe. Depending on the individual model, it is suitable for everyday wear and for special occasions. In short, the style is a must for every gentleman's wardrobe.

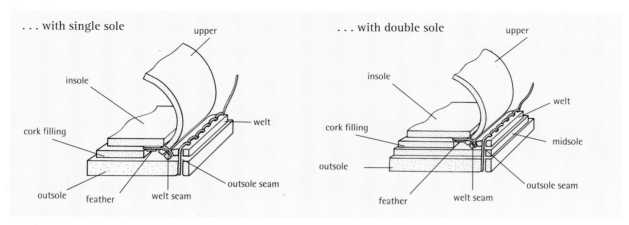

Cross-section of single-soled welted shoe. The first seam joins upper, welt, and insole; the second seam joins the welt to the outsole.

Cross-section of double-soled welted shoe. The second seam joins welt, midsole and outsole.

The Double-stitched Shoe

Both variants of the double-stitched shoe – with a single sole and two rows of stitching, or with a double sole and three rows of stitching – are sturdy, sporty models. However, they can give a touch of elegance to casual daytime clothing. The double-stitched shoe is not suitable for very formal occasions.

There are two common variants of double-stitched shoes: in the first, the welt runs as usual around the shoe from the front of the heel and back again, while in the second the welt surrounds the heel too. In this case the heel area looks broader than usual.

Double-stitched shoes are made of smooth, strong leather, or of leather with a rough surface. Color combinations are frequent. Models coming up over the ankles or made as ankle boots are popular.

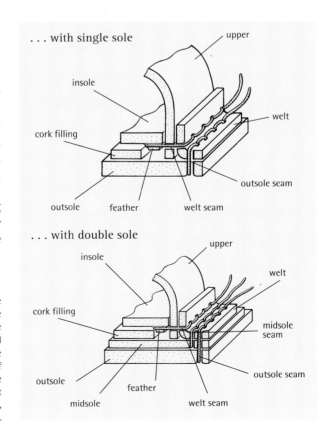

... with single sole

... with double sole

Cross-section of a double-stitched shoe with single and double sole. The stitches of the single-soled shoe run around the welt in two seams. The seams, staggered and interwoven, are more than twice as long as in the welted shoe. The welt seam holds the insole, welt, and upper together, and is not covered but remains fully visible. The sole seam joins the welt to the outsole. In the double-soled double-stitched shoe, there are three rows of stitches running along the outside of the shoe. The welt seam has the same function as in the single-soled shoe. The midsole seam holds the welt and midsole together, and finally the outsole seam joins the welt, midsole, and outsole. All the seams are visible on the outside.

Pit Tanning

All the lower parts of the classic handmade gentleman's shoe – the insole, outsole (and midsole in double-soled shoes), counter, heel, and welt – are traditionally made of strong leather that guarantees a certain durability. Cattle hide prepared by the pit-tanning method, using vegetable substances, has these qualities. The leather for the lower parts of the shoe goes through the same phases of preparation for tanning as leather for the uppers (see page 93). However, there are considerable differences in the tanning process itself. First, different substances are used for tanning; and second, the technique is different. While the hides for the uppers are turned in huge tanning vats, this method cannot be used for sole leather, since the constant movement would soften it up, impairing its durability and the adhesive qualities of the collagen it contains – a feature to be avoided in sole leather because of the particular strains to which it will be subjected. As a result, the ancient method of pit tanning is still used today. At least three pits – sometimes more – are necessary. The hides, cleaned both inside and outside, are steeped for six weeks in the first pit in a tanning liquid containing relatively few tanning agents. They spend another six weeks in the second pit, in a more strongly concentrated solution. Finally, they soak for eleven months more in the third pit. The tanner layers the hides alternately with the vegetable tanning agents. Once the pit is full it is topped up with tanning solution until the layers are completely covered. Now a mysterious process begins in the covered pits, transforming raw animal hides into hard, massive, natural-colored sole leather, resistant to water and high temperatures and easily worked. No artificially made substance can compare with it as yet, although no doubt scientists are at present trying to synthesize leather. Perhaps it will not be too long before they succeed, or perhaps they never will.

The cleaned skins are lowered into the first tanning pit.

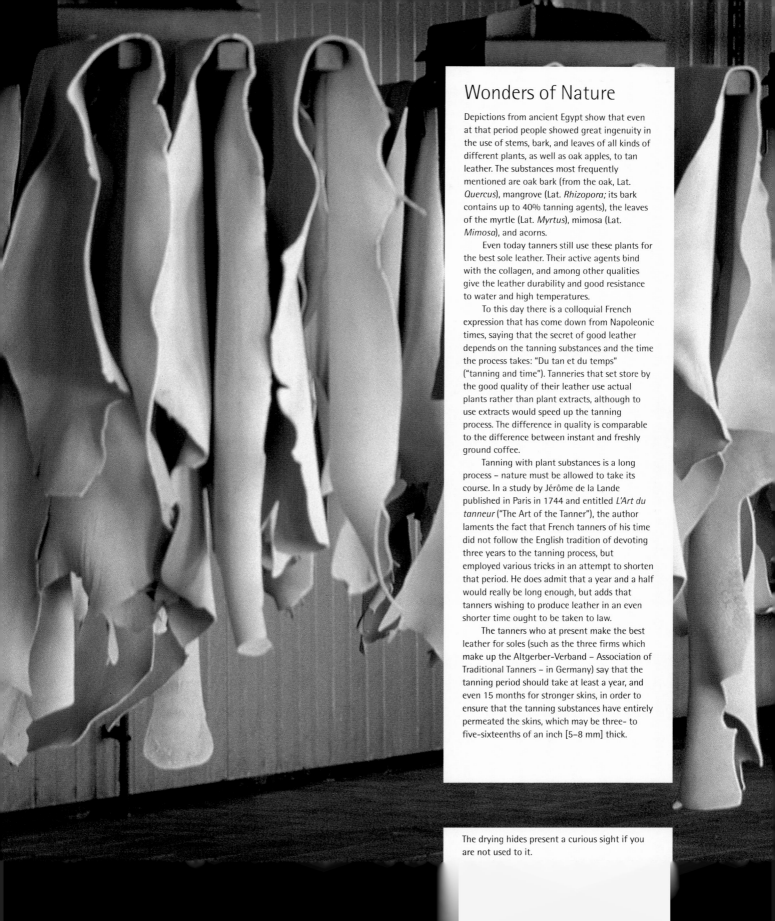

Wonders of Nature

Depictions from ancient Egypt show that even at that period people showed great ingenuity in the use of stems, bark, and leaves of all kinds of different plants, as well as oak apples, to tan leather. The substances most frequently mentioned are oak bark (from the oak, Lat. *Quercus*), mangrove (Lat. *Rhizopora;* its bark contains up to 40% tanning agents), the leaves of the myrtle (Lat. *Myrtus*), mimosa (Lat. *Mimosa*), and acorns.

Even today tanners still use these plants for the best sole leather. Their active agents bind with the collagen, and among other qualities give the leather durability and good resistance to water and high temperatures.

To this day there is a colloquial French expression that has come down from Napoleonic times, saying that the secret of good leather depends on the tanning substances and the time the process takes: "Du tan et du temps" ("tanning and time"). Tanneries that set store by the good quality of their leather use actual plants rather than plant extracts, although to use extracts would speed up the tanning process. The difference in quality is comparable to the difference between instant and freshly ground coffee.

Tanning with plant substances is a long process – nature must be allowed to take its course. In a study by Jérôme de la Lande published in Paris in 1744 and entitled *L'Art du tanneur* ("The Art of the Tanner"), the author laments the fact that French tanners of his time did not follow the English tradition of devoting three years to the tanning process, but employed various tricks in an attempt to shorten that period. He does admit that a year and a half would really be long enough, but adds that tanners wishing to produce leather in an even shorter time ought to be taken to law.

The tanners who at present make the best leather for soles (such as the three firms which make up the Altgerber-Verband – Association of Traditional Tanners – in Germany) say that the tanning period should take at least a year, and even 15 months for stronger skins, in order to ensure that the tanning substances have entirely permeated the skins, which may be three- to five-sixteenths of an inch [5–8 mm] thick.

The drying hides present a curious sight if you are not used to it.

Cattle-hide soles stamped out of the leather. This product of the firm of Johannes Rendenbach in Trier, Germany, founded 120 years ago, is regarded as the Mercedes-Benz among sole leathers, and can proudly bear the quality mark of the German Traditional Tanners' Association.

The tanned leather is compressed by metal rollers exerting high pressure.

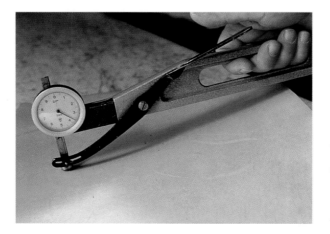

Although quality can be assessed by the color and feel of the leather, it should also be checked with a special instrument. The instrument shown here can measure the thickness of the leather at various points on the hide very precisely.

Leather for the Lower Parts

Craft traditions are followed in different ways and expressed differently from country to country. In Germany, for instance, the triangular quality mark (with a picture of an oak tree at the center) of the Altgerber-Verband, founded in 1930, is a guarantee of traditional pit-tanning methods using active agents from oak trees. This quality mark can be carried only by leather that has achieved its fine quality exclusively through a pit-tanning process with pure vegetable substances and lasting a year. The association is unique in Europe. Only a few individual tanners in Italy, France, Great Britain, and Hungary prepare leather for shoes in a similarly traditional way.

Pit-tanned leather is strong, sturdy but flexible, easily worked, and will stand up without difficulty to the many kinds of stress to which it is subjected during the making and later the wearing of the shoe. It is used for the sole, insole, heel, welt, and counter. Parts of shoes that are made from pit-tanned leather have many advantages. Whether they are worn in rain or snow, on hot tarmac in summer, or on stony ground, pit-tanned leather soles will not lose their shape. The welt will not be inclined to stretch or shrink, but will give the shoe perfect support in all circumstances. The insole breathes particularly well, absorbs sweat from the foot without feeling damp, and has a germicidal effect on bacteria and fungi. The plant substances give the leather an attractive natural color. The smell of well-tanned leather can certainly compete with a good-quality footspray!

The Lower Parts

Large pieces of tanned cattle hide for the lower parts of the shoe are delivered to the shoemaker's workshop by the leather factory, and cut to size by the shoemaker himself. The leather from the neck and belly of the animal, an eighth of an inch [2.5–3.5 mm] thick, is used for the insole, welt, counter, inside toe cap, and the midsole in shoes with double soles. The strongest and sturdiest areas of hide are on the left and right of the animal's backbone, extending from the neck to the small of the back and down to the belly area – on average this section of the hide is a quarter inch [6mm] thick after tanning and preparation. It is also known as butt leather, signifying that it comes from the center of the animal's back. It is particularly suitable for parts of the shoe that will take a great deal of heavy wear, such as the outsole, heel, and rand, while leather from the head, flank, or side of the animal is often used for the heel lifts. While the clicker cuts out the separate parts of the upper in a single operation and then hands them on for further treatment, the shoemaker cuts only the lower parts of the shoe needed for the next step in the process at any one time, since the final measurements of several pieces will be determined only during the construction of the shoe. The whole process requires time and patience.

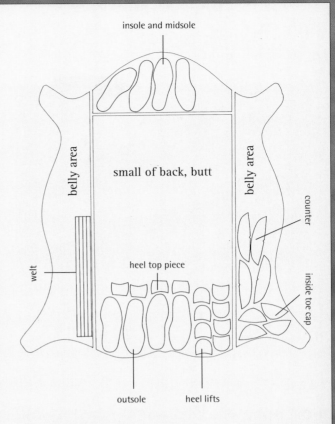

The edge of the neck and belly area of the tanned, prepared hide is thinner than the butt leather. The shoemaker will decide on the suitability of a piece of leather for a part of the shoe on the grounds of its thickness.

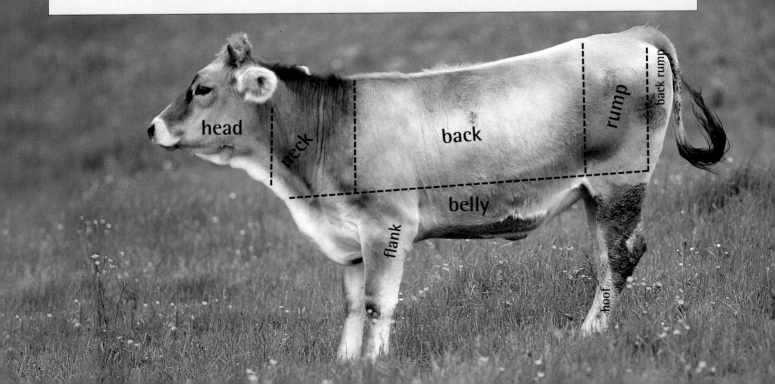

Cutting out the Lower Parts

The knife used for cutting out the lower parts of the shoe is a simple piece of steel. The sharpened blade is slightly twisted so that it will adjust to the leather better during cutting. The handle is covered with several layers of leather to keep the shoemaker from injuring his hand, since he exerts great force in cutting the leather. After each piece is cut out the knife is sharpened on a whetstone, to make working easier and ensure a clean cut.

The leather for the lower part of the shoe is delivered from the tannery suitably cut into neck, belly, and back areas. Separate parts of the shoe are cut out as the operations of making the shoe go along. The shoemaker cuts out only the part he needs next, beginning with the insoles cut from the neck area of the hide. He places his lasts on the leather and carefully traces their outlines on the material. In some cases there may be as much as a whole shoe size in difference between a customer's two feet.

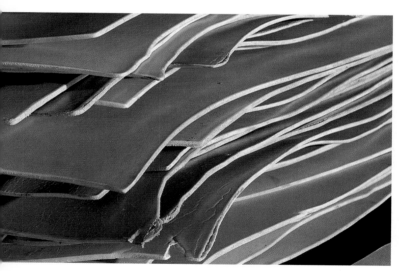

The back of the hide, measuring about a quarter inch [5–6 mm] in thickness, is delivered in rectangular pieces. Even this photograph gives an idea of the strength of the material. This kind of leather will be used several times in the course of the work. The shoemaker cuts out the outsole when the shoe is already half finished. He places the welted shoe on the leather, draws its outline, and cuts the outsole from the leather by the same method as for the insole. The heel lifts come from the butt leather too. Four to six lifts are required for a heel, depending on its height, but the shoemaker will not cut them out until the shoe is already soled, since the soled shoe provides the pattern for the size of these lifts. It is important to perform these various operations in the right order, or else the final outcome will be unsuitable for the customer.

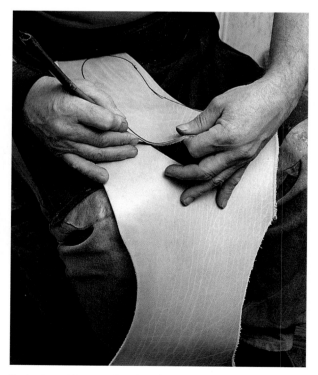

The insole must be strong, but also soft and flexible. The neck area of the hide, an eighth of an inch [2.5–3.5 mm] thick, is suitable for insoles. The shoemaker cuts out the left and right insoles slowly and with great care. The size of the insole determines the length of the welt.

The Insole

The insole is an important linking component of the shoe, since the upper and the welt are fastened to it. The construction of the shoe, as mentioned above, begins with the fitting of the insole.

Once the insole is cut out, the shoemaker shaves a thin layer away from its right side, using a piece of glass passed over it in several powerful movements; the side treated in this way will be on the inside.

The shoemaker then places the last on his knees, sole side up, places the insole, which has been softened in water, on it, and presses it firmly down on the last with his foot-strap. Using pliers, he stretches the sole out well on all sides and fixes it with three to four metal tacks. The heads of the tacks are turned in to give the insole as good a grip on the last as possible (this fastening will be unnecessary at a later stage of the work, when the nails will be removed again). The shoemaker pares the leather away along the edge of the last, pressing the insole firmly down and running the vertically held knife around the edge. He must follow the shape of the last very precisely in this operation.

A sharp piece of glass is a very good tool for smoothing the surface of the insole.

This photograph shows how the shoemaker uses his foot-strap in fixing the insole to the last.

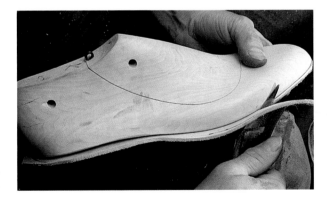

Extra leather is pared away, and the insole is fitted to the shape of the last.

The Foot-strap or Stirrup

The shoemaker needs both hands for most operations involved in making the shoe. He can leave them free by using a foot-strap or stirrup made of stout leather, a half to three-quarters of an inch [1.5–2 cm] wide (today such straps will often roll up automatically). The shoemaker loops this strap around his legs and one foot. He can use his foot to relax or tighten the strap as required while he works.

The Piece of Glass

An ancient, extremely simple tool of traditional shoemaking, and still in use today: a piece of glass from a window pane or bottle with irregular edges is used to shave, taper, and smooth the upper surface of the leather, and to score marks on it. It is a very cheap tool for the shoemaker, since it needs no repairs and can easily be replaced at any time – you might call it a disposable tool!

The Feather

The locations for the heel and the feather are marked on the insole with a pencil or piece of glass. The feather (an area about a quarter of an inch broad and a sixteenth of an inch high [6 mm x 2 mm]) runs around the insole roughly a quarter inch [6 mm] from the edge – on the inside along the shank – however, it is up to a half inch [1 cm] from the edge, since otherwise the wearer of the shoe, who will usually tend to tip his foot inward, would be treading down on the seam too soon. The shoemaker pares away the leather to right and left of the marking with an insole plane, a process known to shoemakers as skiving the insole.

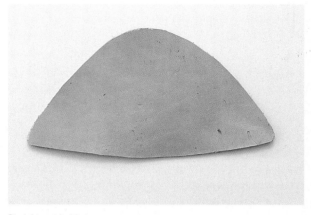

Straight-cut inside toe cap

The leather is pared down or "skived" with a steel insole plane.

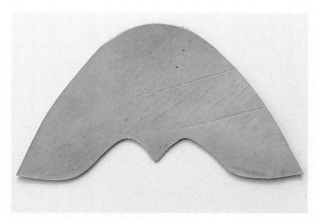

Wing-shaped inside toe cap

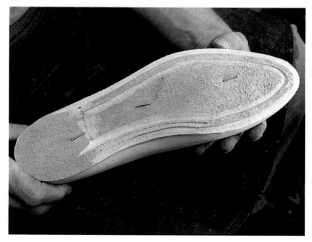

The feather is clearly visible on the insole, now ready for welting.

Toe cap for a slip-on shoe

Preparing the Upper

The shoemaker also does the rest of the work on the assembled and lined upper. He cuts out the reinforcement pieces: the straight or wing-shaped toe cap comes from the neck or belly area of the hide, the counter from the edge of the belly area and the side reinforcements from small pieces of the leather used for the uppers. Then the edges are tapered and coated with adhesive on both sides. At the toe of the shoe, the inside toe cap is inserted between the upper and the lining leather, the inside counter is inserted at the heel, and the side reinforcements go in along the sides. Exerting strong pressure with his hand, the shoemaker first presses down on the outer sides of the upper spread out on the bench, then on the lining side, so that the adhesive will be evenly spread and the surfaces will stick together well. It is obvious at first sight whether a shoe has been made with or without a toe cap, which forms a strong, firm, protective covering over the toes. Its dome should be large enough for the toes to have plenty of space

underneath, so that they do not come into contact with the hard leather surface even when the whole weight of the body rests on the foot during walking and the foot is extended within the shoe.

Toe caps are never the same thickness all over. Because of the stress exerted on it, the leather should be thickest at the tip of the shoe, retaining all its original thickness at this point. The leather then becomes thinner toward the middle of the shoe, where the movement of the foot calls for more flexibility. The shoemaker pares the leather away first with a sharp knife, then with a file and a piece of glass, so that it gradually tapers down to a thickness of about a fiftieth of an inch [0.5 mm].

The application of adhesive also affects the strength of the toe of the shoe; glue is spread rather more thickly over the toe area itself, more thinly toward the middle of the foot. The glue itself and the amount applied have a stiffening and strengthening function, which are ultimately very important for the finished shoe.

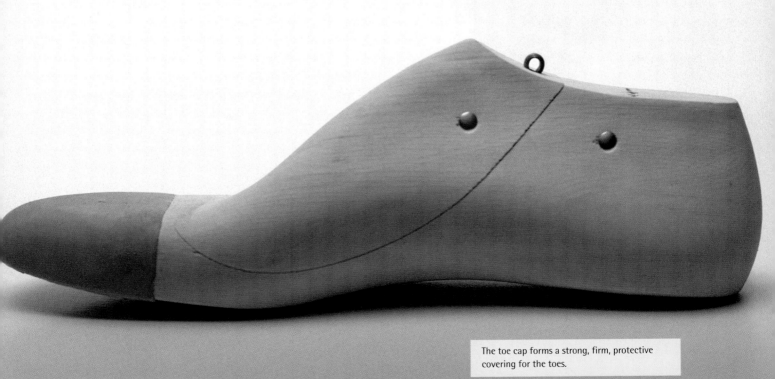

The toe cap forms a strong, firm, protective covering for the toes.

The Counter

The inside counter must be tapered at its upper and lower ends to give better flexibility and a good fit at the heel.

When the side parts of the shoe are assembled this reinforcing section gives the heel the firm support required for putting shoes on and taking them off, as well as for walking, and prevents the relatively thin leather of the upper from breaking here. As an extension of the heel, the counter also gives the foot stability in the shoe. Its thickness tapers away gradually from the edge of the sole upward, and it is fitted between the upper and the lining so that its top edge comes to the top of the upper – if it ended lower down, the leather of the upper would crease. The counter is made in the same way as the toe cap, and it should also be strong and firm to withstand pressure.

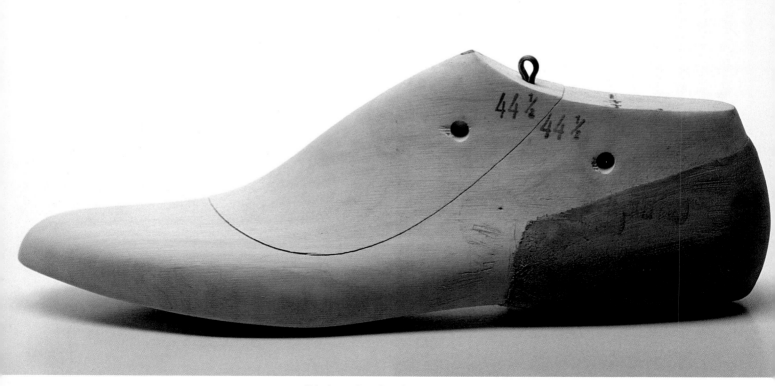

This picture shows how the tapered inside counter fits on the last. It is inserted between the lining and the upper, and all three layers of leather are pulled together on the last.

The Side Reinforcements

Their function is to give support to the inside and outside of the shoe, and to prevent the leather from stretching and creasing while the wearer walks. The side reinforcements are made from pieces of the leather used for the uppers, and are about a twentieth of an inch [1.2–1.4 mm] thick.

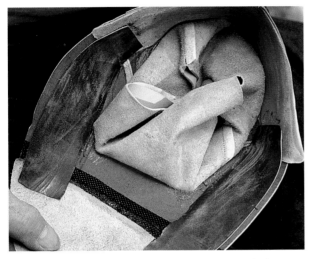

The lining leather is pulled in and folded over so that it is not in the way while the inside toe cap and counter and the side reinforcements, glued on both sides, are inserted. These reinforcement sections are joined to each other.

After the reinforcements are in place, the shoemaker folds the lining leather back again and smooths out the three layers of leather, which are now stuck together. The leather of the lining is powdered to make it easier to remove the last when the shoe is finished.

The Adhesive

Tradition-conscious shoemakers make their own adhesive – from flour, chestnuts, or potatoes. Dried leaves of this adhesive are dissolved in the correct quantity of water and stirred to form a glue that can easily be applied. It takes great skill to judge the right amount of water correctly. If the glue is too thin it will run too much, and if it is too thick it may form lumps. The shoemaker must also make sure he does not apply too much glue to the pieces of leather, or when the inside toe cap, counter, and side reinforcements are inserted it may seep through the upper or even the leather lining, leaving unattractive marks. It cannot be said that this never happens, but a true craftsman will take great care to avoid it.

The glue is made of flour, chestnuts, or potatoes, and is mixed with water. The shoemaker makes it himself, keeping his own recipe a secret.

Lasting

Now that the shoemaker has fitted the insole to the sole area of the last, concluding the preparatory work, the important second phase of constructing the shoe can begin: it must be shaped with a pair of pliers.

The essential aim of this complicated operation is to give the stitched upper a rounded form like the shape of the last. Particular care has to be taken when shaping the toe cap and heel areas, where there are folds in the leather on the last. These folds must now be smoothed away and curved into shape.

The shoemaker now works from the sole side of the shoe. He pulls the upper forward with the grooved pliers, beginning with the area around the ball of the foot on both inside and outside, and at the same time he tautens the leather. As it is pulled forward the shoe begins to take shape.

The shoemaker's pliers shown here have two functions: the grooving of their jaws pulls and smooths the leather of the upper, and the shoemaker also uses the squared area projecting from the pliers on one side to knock tacks in. He can thus complete two operations at the same time with one tool: first he pulls the leather taut, and next he can nail it down.

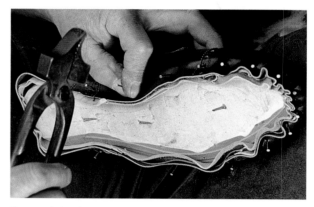

The upper is first fastened with eight metal tacks – three at the toe cap, two at each side, and one at the heel – so that it will not slip about on the last. The shoemaker begins stretching the leather to shape with the pliers, applying them at intervals of about 2 inches [5–6 cm]. He bends the leather over to the insole and fixes it again with metal nails. Now and then the shoemaker turns the last over to see if the upper has shifted away from the central axis.

The right length for the metal nails or tacks used in the operation of shaping with pliers is 1 inch [2.5 cm], and their diameter is about a twentieth of an inch [1.2–1.4 mm]. It is important that they do not break or bend as they are knocked in. A good shoemaker can knock in a nail with a single blow right through the three layers of leather and another three-sixteenths of an inch [5 mm] into the last.

This photograph shows that all three layers of the upper – now stretched to shape – are rather longer than necessary. The extra leather will be pared away all around with a knife, so that the edge of the upper fits closely to the feather.

Hammering the Shoe

The upper is now carefully and skillfully hammered with the disk-shaped end of the cobbler's hammer (which weighs about 1 pound [500 g]). In this operation the shoemaker compresses the fibers of the leather, thus improving the shape and hardwearing capacity of the shoe. The material of the last is important here: a good-quality wood will vibrate in time to the hammer blows and match the rhythm automatically, almost as if it came to life under the incessant blows of the shoemaker's hammer.

The shoemaker's hammer resembles an ordinary domestic hammer, but is used in more ways: one end of the hammer head ends in a rather blunted peen. Any wrinkles between two tacks can be smoothed out with this surface. The other end of the hammer head is a flat disk. It is used to hammer the sides of the shoe and remove any wrinkles in the leather entirely. The shoemaker works on the upper side of the counter and the toe cap in the same way, to ensure a smooth fit with the rest of the upper. The third surface employed is the handle of the hammer itself, which is used to level out the sole once it has been stitched on.

Dozens of nails stick out of the last and look like hedgehog prickles. They are bent over toward the central axis of the last with the hammer, so that they lie down flat on it.

After using his pliers the shoemaker carefully hammers the leather of the upper to fit the three-dimensional shape of the last.

A perfect row of small, regular stitches is typical of the welted shoe.

The Welted Shoe

Preparing the Welt

The welt is cut from the belly area of the hide, and consists of leather strips three-quarters of an inch [18 mm] wide and an eighth of an inch [3 mm] thick. The hide from this area is very sturdy and thick, but also flexible.

The leather strips are soaked in water and then kept damp overnight, wrapped in paper, to soften the leather. The welt can be worked much more easily when it is softened like this. (When the leather dries out at the end of the welting operation it will regain its original sturdy quality.) The shoemaker cuts one side of the welt away with a knife held at an angle of 45° so that the strip of leather will fit to the feather of the insole. He scores a channel about a twentieth of an inch [1mm] thick in the welt with a piece of glass. The stitches will be set here at a later stage in this complicated process of making a new shoe.

The welt is cut at an angle of 45° on one side.

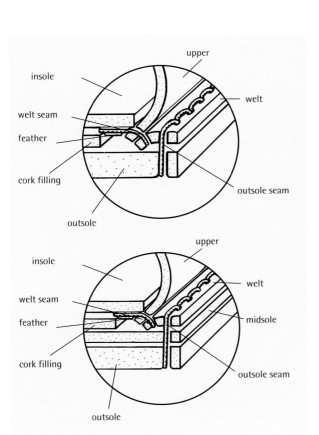

This welt has been cut to the right measurements and marked with a stitching channel.

The welt seam holds the insole, upper, and welt together. It is invisible, since the outsole will cover it later. The outsole seam itself, which fixes the welt and outsole (in a single-soled shoe) or the welt, midsole, and outsole (in a double-soled shoe) is visible from outside.

Cobbler's Thread

To stitch the welt, the shoemaker uses a thread measuring about 8 feet [2 m] made of 12 strands (or for a very sturdy shoe up to 24 strands) of linen or hemp, regularly twisted and of the appropriate strength. Hemp is preferred because it will absorb more cobbler's wax and thus seal the join better. The strands are not usually cut straight from the original thread, but are spliced out so that the tip can be twisted to as smooth and firm a texture as possible. The shoemaker treats the thread with cobbler's wax mixed by himself, to give the seam a good, waterproof seal. He warms resin, beeswax, and paraffin together, pours the melted mixture into cold water, and after a short cooling period he kneads the mixture into small rolls through which he draws the thread – working as fast as possible so that the wax, warmed in the hand, does not cool down again. The wax particles cling regularly to the thread, surrounding it like a coating and holding the fibers together.

The shoemaker cuts a piece 8 feet [2 m] long off the roll of thread. He divides it up into its 12 strands and sharpens the end of each, much as one sharpens a pencil. Then he twists the 12 strands together into a thread again. The end of the thread is now pointed enough to pass easily through the eye of the needle.

The shoemaker pulls the thread, 8 feet [2 m] in length through the cobbler's wax several times, to make it waterproof and durable.

The shoemaker mixes his own cobbler's wax from resin, beeswax, and paraffin wax, and shapes the mixture into little rolls.

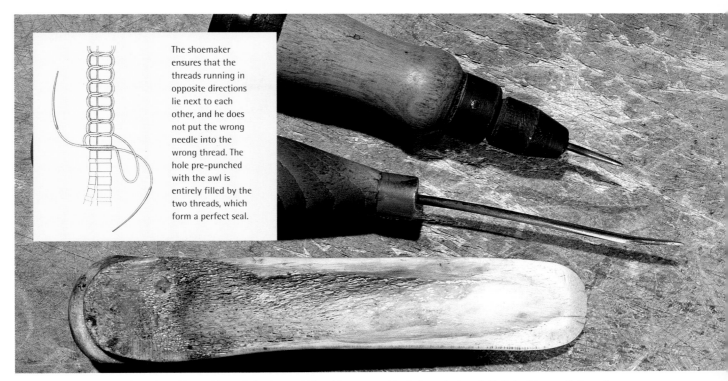

The shoemaker ensures that the threads running in opposite directions lie next to each other, and he does not put the wrong needle into the wrong thread. The hole pre-punched with the awl is entirely filled by the two threads, which form a perfect seal.

Tools used for sewing the welt are the welting awl (center), the short awl (above) for pre-punching holes, and a bone knife (below) to smooth the welt.

The Seam

In welt-sewn shoes, the seam joining the upper and the insole is stitched first. This seam is not visible on the outside. It is particularly important to set the stitches of the seam firmly and regularly, because they have a great effect on the durability of the shoe. Exhibits in shoe museums all over the world show that careful stitching has always been highly valued. It is quite usual to see shoes over a hundred years old on display, with leather that may be worn and cracking, but with their seams still in perfect condition.

Two welting needles are used to stitch the welt. The needles are straight, 3 inches [8 cm] long and about a twentieth of an inch [0.5–0.8 mm] in diameter. To make his work easier, the shoemaker warms them over a flame and bends them into a slight curve with a pair of pliers. Then he warms the thread, which has been sealed with wax and sharpened to a point, threads the needle, and prepares the awls and bone knife for the ensuing operations. Using his welting awl, he punches the hole through which the needle will then pull the thread. Stitching must be done fast, so that the wax coating of

the warmed thread does not cool down again. A good shoemaker must be able to rely on the accuracy of his eye, and a great many skilled movements, to ensure that the stitches are regular. This ability only comes after years of practice and patient repetition of the range of tasks involved in making shoes.

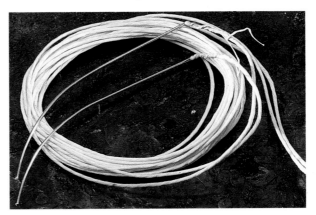

The shoemaker requires two straight needles 3 inches [8 cm] in length for stitching the welt. This is easier if they are warmed and then bent.

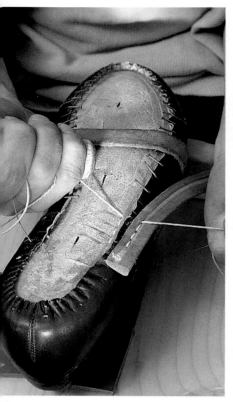

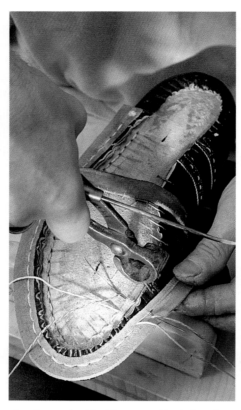

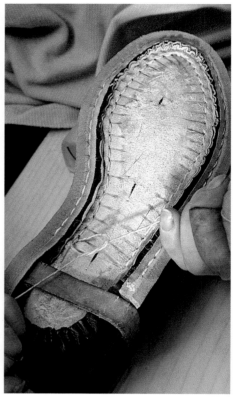

Stitching the welt: the shoemaker begins at the heel, and works toward the big toe.

Once the seam has joined the upper and insole, the nails can be removed one by one.

The seam finishes back at the level of the heel, opposite its start, and the two threads are firmly knotted.

Stitching the Welt

"Small stitches do their job, big stitches earn your bread." This old German shoemaker's proverb points up the necessity of small stitches for a durable, hardwearing shoe, and at the same time comments ruefully that the shoemaker can make more money by working fast – in this case, by using big stitches. The stitches of a welted shoe are usually a quarter inch [6 mm] long. Those of a double-stitched shoe are longer – around three-eighths of an inch [1 cm] – but since this kind of shoe has three rows of stitches instead of two, the stitching is just as stable (see page 157).

The shoemaker places the welt against the upper and the insole along the line of the feather and stitches it in place, beginning at the heel and working toward the toe cap. The insole, welt and upper are pierced with the awl, which passes through the feather. As the shoemaker sews, he draws the thread up from underneath with one needle, and then down through the same hole from above with the other needle. After every stitch he pulls the threads tight so that the stitches will be taut and embed themselves in the leather. He protects his fingers from injury during this operation with a small leather protector. In order to exert even more force, the shoemaker winds the thread over the awl and pulls it tight. As soon as he has made a couple of stitches he pulls out the nails, whose function has now been taken over by the stitches. Once the seam is in place all the way around, there are no nails left. After the last stitch has been made, both threads are tied in a good knot and the ends of the threads are cut.

The upper is always cut longer and the welt wider than necessary, to facilitate the stitching of the seam. When the stitching is finished the shoemaker trims the extra leather away. He compresses the material with light hammer blows and adjusts the welt with his pliers. Any traces left by the pliers are removed with the bone knife.

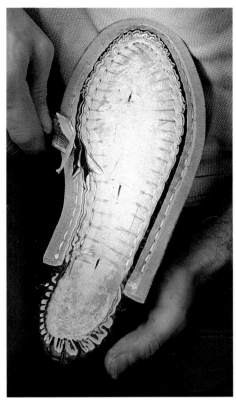

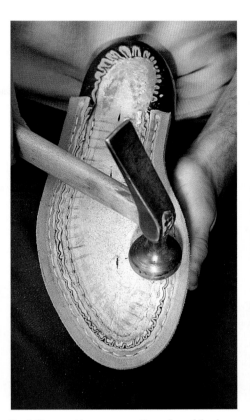

The shoemaker trims the extra leather away from the upper and the welt, working carefully so as not to damage the seam.

Careful hammer blows compress the surface of the shoe, particularly at the welt and the seam.

Pliers are used to adjust the welt and prepare for the stitching of the outsole seam.

The welt is smoothed with the bone knife.

Completing the Welt: the Rand

A strip of leather matching the breadth of the welt, with small triangles cut into it so that it can follow the curve of the heel, completes the welt and facilitates the next operation, the fitting of the outsole. Another function of this strip, known as the rand, is to hold the shoe together; the welt has been carefully stitched and the rand fixed with wooden pegs which are driven right through the layers of the insole, the upper (now fitted in place), the counter, and the lining. The width and thickness of the rand are the same as in the welt.

After the rand has been tacked to the heel area of the insole with several wooden pegs, the shoemaker cuts it to the correct length. When it is finally fastened in place, the holes for these pegs are compressed: a wooden peg is knocked into holes pre-punched by a rather short awl at intervals of about a quarter inch [6–7 mm], with a little glue applied to them. The hole made by the awl is always smaller than the diameter of the wooden peg, so that it will fit snugly and hold the material together well. The projecting ends of the wooden pegs are then filed down.

The wooden pegs are made of birch, hornbeam, or beech. Birchwood pegs are usually preferred since they can be split downward quite easily, but are difficult to break across, so it is easy to work with them. The length of the wooden pegs fixing the rand is usually about a half inch [14 mm], and their diameter three-sixteenths of an inch [4 mm].

The shoemaker pre-punches the holes with an awl.

The rand is fixed in place with wooden pegs and trimmed to the correct length.

The wooden pegs must be placed close to each other to ensure stability.

Regular stitching shows the course of the seam along the feather.

Soling the Shoe

A hollow space between the insole and outsole would be created by the thicknesses of the upper, rand, and welt. To prevent this, and to give the shoe more stability, a shank spring is fitted, while the rest of the hollow area is filled with layers of cork.

Depending on the model, a welted shoe may have a single or a double sole. In a single-soled shoe, the outsole is stitched directly to the welt. In its double-soled variant, a midsole thinner than the outsole itself, cut from the edge of the neck area of the hide, is glued to the welt and the interlining before the outsole is fitted to the shoe. The shoemaker then stitches the three layers of leather together.

Both approaches require a steady hand to ensure that the end-result is satisfactory.

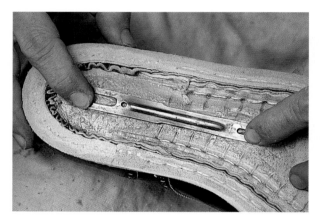

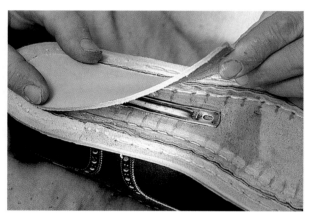

Only the front third of the shoe should bend when the wearer is walking. The sole and heel must remain stable at every step, preventing the heel from wobbling and giving the foot good support. This is achieved by means of a steel spring, known as a shank spring, set in the hollow area of the sole and running from halfway along the heel to the beginning of the ball of the foot, at the shank area of the sole. The length of the spring depends on the size of the shoe, its sturdiness and flexibility, and the model of the shoe itself. It is held in place in the insole by a leather covering fixed with wooden pegs.

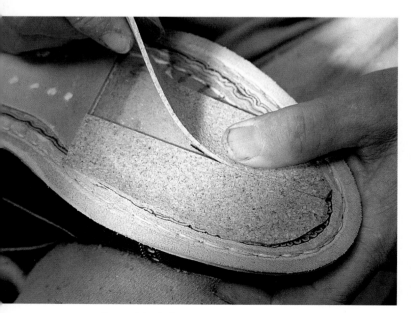

The remaining hollow part of the shoe is filled with light, flexible layers of cork for stability and comfort.

The cover of the shank spring and the cork lining fill up the space between the soles. The shoemaker levels off the surface with a file.

The leather soles cut from the hide are soaked in water, like the welt, and then kept damp wrapped in newspaper for 24 hours, to make them easier to handle during the fitting operation.

The shoemaker roughens the surfaces to be stuck together with a file to make them more adhesive. He must take particular care not to damage any of the stitches in the process.

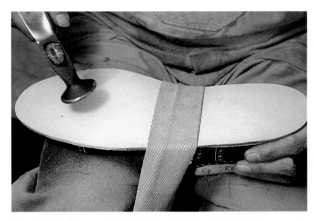

The glued sole is pressed firmly in place with the shaft of the hammer and then hammered with the disk end of the head, to compress the adhesive and the glued areas. The shoemaker uses his foot-strap to hold the shoe in place on his thigh.

Regular pressure exerted by pliers all the way around the shoe joins the welt and the sole, pressing the adhesive into the leather. The shoemaker trims away excess leather at the edge of the sole with a knife – soles cut by hand from leather are always a little larger than their final size – and adjusts the edges of the welt and sole to each other.

The Outsole

In the welted shoe only a single row of stitching on the shoe – between the front of the sole and the heel – shows that the welt and outsole are not just stuck but also stitched together. This seam is covered by the flap of the stitching channel on the sole side.

The outsole is scored with a piece of glass about a quarter inch [5–6 mm] from the edge of the sole, and a cut is made with a sharp knife to halfway through the thickness of the sole along the marked line. This cut is pared away with a scraper and deepened to make a channel. The shoe now has a small leather edge, the flap of the stitching channel, which must not be broken off or damaged during the operation, since it is to cover the stitches after they are set in place.

The shoemaker must keep a careful watch on the correct depth and breadth of the channel, to ensure that the stitches are protected from possible wear and tear (they would not be if the channel were too shallow), and the sole does not break up (it would if the channel were too deep). In addition, the threads must lie close to each other in the channel, occupying its entire width, so that the seam is well closed and adequately covered. As always, these details are crucial to the successful completion of the making of the shoe.

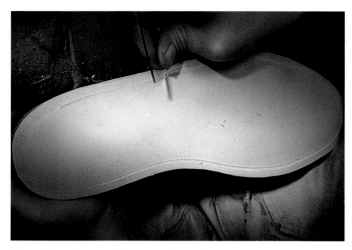

The mark is pared away with a scraper, deepened to form a channel, and smoothed with a bone knife. The outsole seam will run along this channel.

The scraper, used to pare away the leather and deepen the groove.

The shoemaker scores the outsole to a depth of half its thickness.

A bone knife – in this case with a point – made by the shoemaker himself.

Marking Stitches on the Outsole

In stitching the welt, insole, and upper together the shoemaker relies on his eye. This seam remains invisible inside the shoe and has only a functional role, so that while its stitches do have to be accurately placed, experience and a trained eye are enough to do the job. If the shoemaker sets the stitches close enough and pulls the threads tight, the seam will be sufficiently durable.

On the outside of the welt, the seam holding welt and insole together has an esthetic function too; this row of perfectly regular stitches is an ornament to the shoe. The places for the stitches are therefore pre-marked before the welt and the outsole are stitched together.

For this purpose the shoemaker uses a stitch marker, a metal tool with two rounded teeth and a curved hollow between them. It is pressed firmly down on the welt, and the teeth leave dot-shaped impressions on the leather. The shoemaker passes the stitch marker all around the welt, marking the place for each individual stitch. In welted shoes the distance between stitches is about a quarter inch [6.6 mm]. The points marked must lie so that the tip of the awl, set precisely on the mark, will come through into the channel and nowhere else when forced through the many layers of leather. The depth of the layers of leather to be pierced with the awl can be up to a third of an inch [9 mm] for a single sole, and up to as much as a half inch [12 mm] for a double sole.

The stitch marker pre-marks the places for the stitches of the welt.

The layers of leather are punched with the awl, which comes through into the channel.

The stitch marker has two rounded teeth with a curved hollow between them. It fulfills two functions: marking the places for the welt awl and the needle, and smoothing the stitch marks later. The depth of the leather it must penetrate is up to a third of an inch [9 mm] for a single-soled shoe, up to a half inch [12 mm] for a double-soled shoe.

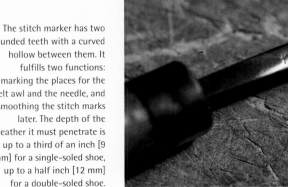

Double-stitching

The stitching technique used in soling the shoe is the same as in stitching the welt, insole, and upper together. The cobbler's thread, well coated with wax – the water-repellent resinous coating is even more important on the sole – is threaded through the eyes of curved needles and pulled through the pre-punched holes in opposite directions.

Completing the Welt-stitching

The marks made in advance by the stitch marker leave the shoemaker free to concentrate on the regularity of his seam. In addition, he must ensure that the threads are pulled through with the same amount of force, since none of the stitches must be too loose, or any tighter than necessary. After the last stitch the ends of the threads are firmly tied in a knot. In stitching the outsole the shoemaker must be particularly careful not to damage the flap of the stitching channel, which will be closed in the next operation. Once the sole leather is holding the seam enclosed, it will have regained its original thickness, ready for the next stage.

The stitching channel is filled with glue and closed with the flap. The shoemaker uses the angular side of his hammer head to close up the sole leather, which is still damp and easily shaped. Once the leather has dried out, all that will show of the seam is a very thin line.

To ensure perfect regularity in the outer seam, the shoemaker runs the stitch marker along it. The little teeth of the tool grip the thread between the stitches and pull them slightly upward, so that they now sit on top of the welt like little beads.

A single tool is used to compress the leather of the sole – the hammer. Its three functions are clearly illustrated here: the angular peen closes and smooths over the flap of the stitching channel, the disk-shaped head hammers not only the channel but the entire sole, compressing the material and smoothing out any bumps or hollows. Finally, the shaft of the hammer is pressed down hard and drawn along the sole several times, to close the channel entirely. The result is a perfectly smooth surface.

The special feature of the double-stitched shoe is an interestingly emphasized welt, with strong rows of stitching.

The Double-stitched Shoe

A single-soled double-stitched shoe has two rows of strong stitching; a double-soled double-stitched shoe (the kind usually preferred) has three rows. The following pages illustrate the process of welting double-soled shoes step by step. In both welted and double-stitched shoes, the function of the welt is to hold the upper, insole, and outsole together. The difference between the two types of shoe is in the amount of emphasis on the welt and the stitching. Unlike the more elegant, lightweight welted shoe, the welt and seams of the double-stitched shoe have an esthetic as well as a structural function. They are emphasized as ornamentation on a rather sporty, robust type of shoe.

There is one major difference between the two kinds of shoes in the preparations for stitching. A welt about seven-eighths of an inch [22 mm] wide is cut for the double-stitched shoe, three-sixteenths of an inch [4 mm] broader than for the welted shoe. The rest of the preparations are much the same: the insole is fixed to the lower side of the last, the assembled upper is fitted to it, nailed to the last, and the nails are turned in. The process is illustrated in these photographs, which show the differences and similarities between the two approaches.

The edge of the broad welt is shaved down with a knife firmly held at an angle of 45°.

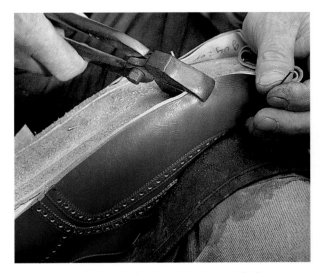

The feather is worked into the insole, and the shaping with pliers can begin. This process is exactly the same as in the welted shoe. The upper is fixed to the insole and the last with metal nails.

In the case of a last with a particularly high domed area at the toe of the shoe, the toe cap is not nailed on with the upper, but separately. The next operation is to stretch the upper part of the toe of the shoe, to prevent the leather from developing creases.

The Welt Seam

The awl is used to punch through the welt, upper, and insole. The thread, consisting of 12 strands of fibers – up to 24 in very sturdy shoes – is pulled through these holes in opposite directions with two needles. The length of a stitch in the double-stitched shoe is up to a half inch [10 mm]. The seam shows on the outside.

The nails can be progressively removed as the seam, now pulled tight, joins the upper to the welt. Stitching is relatively fast because of the large stitches, and the nails are rapidly pulled out as work proceeds.

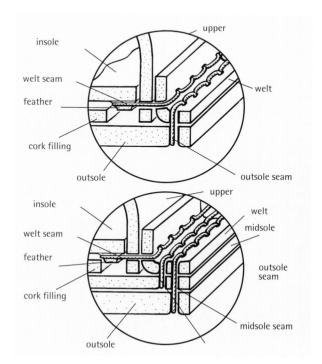

The diagram shows which parts of the various seams – the welt seam, midsole seam, and outsole seam – hold which parts of the shoe together. All the seams show on the outside.

Here the welt runs all the way around the shoe, with its ends meeting each other at the heel. The welt is turned into the horizontal at an angle of 90° with pliers.

Preparing for the Second Row of Stitching

Before the shoemaker begins on the second row of stitching, he must prepare in the same way as for the welted shoe (see page 143 ff.). He inserts a shank spring, a piece of leather, and the cork filling into the hollow area on the insole. Then he hammers the cork filling slightly to distribute the adhesive well over it. A double-soled shoe is considerably more comfortable when the wearer is walking, since the extra midsole cushions the foot better against any irregularities in the ground. This sole, about an eighth of an inch [3–4 mm] thick, is thinner than the outsole and thus more flexible. The surface of the leather is slightly roughened to help the adhesive to cling better, and is then coated with glue and stuck to the layer of leather, the shank spring, and the cork filling. The shoemaker presses the midsole down hard on the adhesive with the hammer head. The shoe is now ready for the second row of stitching.

The shank spring in the midsole area is covered with a layer of leather.

The shank spring is then fastened in place with wooden pegs.

The welt, the cork filling of the midsole area, and the layer of leather are coated with adhesive.

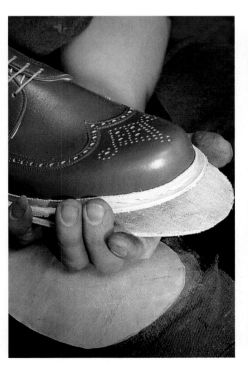

The midsole is glued in place. This photograph shows how the welt, bent into the horizontal, is pressed against the upper and the midsole.

Strong pressure with the hammer head fixes the midsole in place.

The Midsole Seam   The Outsole Seam

The second row of stitching joins the welt and the midsole, which are already held together by adhesive. The shoemaker punches through these layers of leather with his awl, and then pulls the thread through from different directions, using two needles. Each stitch of this sole seam begins in the middle of one of the stitches in the first row; the seams thus run parallel, but the stitches themselves are staggered by three-sixteenths of an inch [5 mm]. The effect is to distribute the load on the shoe more evenly: if the foot rolls during walking the two seams will not take the strain at the same time, but in a kind of wave movement.

While the shoemaker is constructing the shoe, he must take care not to damage the seams. However, they are protected in various ways: the welt seam is less vulnerable because of its position; the midsole welt seam is covered by the outsole; and the outsole seam is hidden under the flap of the stitching channel. There is therefore little danger of any serious harm being caused.

The third row of stitching has to hold together three layers of leather amounting to a thickness of up to a half inch [12 mm] (depending on the sturdiness of the shoe, and in particular of the outsole): they are the welt, the midsole, and the outsole. The last named is cut from a piece of butt leather about a quarter inch [6 mm] thick, and fixed to the midsole with adhesive. The soling method for the double-stitched shoe is the same as for the welted shoe (see page 150 ff.). A stitching channel and flap are worked into the outsole about an eighth of an inch [2–3 mm] from the edge (depending on the width of the welt), and holes are pre-punched in this groove with the awl. Piercing the layers of leather with the awl is not an easy task even in a welted shoe, and calls for considerable force. The holes punched for the third row of stitching must be accessible from the outsole side so that the stitches run parallel to the second row of stitching, and are set symmetrically with the first row of stitching – yet another challenge to the shoemaker's skills.

The welt seam and outsole seam stitches, a half inch [10 mm] in length, run parallel but are staggered by three-sixteenths of an inch [5 mm].

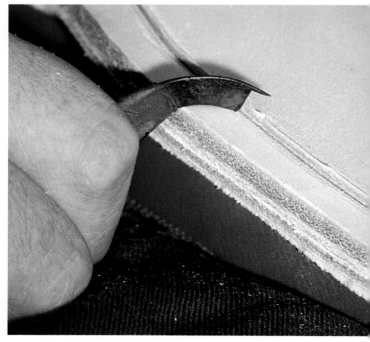

The mark scored in the outsole is shaved away, and the stitching channel is ready for the outsole seam.

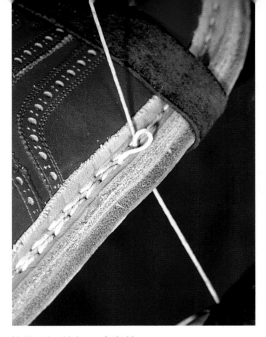

Making the third row of stitching.

The edge of the outsole is adjusted to the midsole.

After the seam is covered by the flap of the stitching, the outsole is also fixed and ornamented with copper nails.

The double-soled double-stitched shoe is ready for the heel to be fitted.

The Heel

The shoe heel was invented in Persia in the twelfth century AD to give horsemen a better grip on the stirrup, and allow them to rise in the saddle during battle. It spread very slowly to Europe by way of Turkey (where the first finds date from AD 1350) and Hungary. It is likely that fashion-conscious Frenchmen were wearing high-heeled shoes in the sixteenth century, but the first documentary record of such shoes is in a price list of 1605. At this time, heels were probably still just a wooden wedge set between the heel of the foot and the sole, serving to make the wearer look taller rather than to stabilize the foot. But it was not long before heels fitted on the outside of the shoe were introduced. They were at their most extreme in size and ornamentation during the baroque period. Heels that were often much too high prevented the foot from being held naturally and unbalanced the shoe. After 1800 heels went out of fashion again, and flat, lightweight silk shoes were worn for two or three decades.

Such whims of fashion are a thing of the past (at least in gentlemen's shoes), but the heel is still with us. Today both shoemakers and the wearers of shoes have realized that because of the anatomy of the foot, a well-shaped heel of suitable height acts as a support during both standing and walking, ensures regular distribution of weight between the toes and the heel, and increases the flexibility of the shoe.

Louis XIV of France wore high heels to make himself look taller (painting of the king in royal robes, Hyacinthe Rigaud, 1701, now in the Louvre, Paris).

Till the 17th century, heels were confined to riding boots. From the baroque period onward elegant models – like this brocade shoe – had heels as well (Bally Schuhmuseum, Schönenwerd).

The most comfortable shape of heel is slightly asymmetrical.

A trapezoid heel widening slightly below is suitable for sturdy, broad-toed shoes.

A narrow-toed shoe should have a trapezoid heel tapering slightly below.

The Correct Measurement

In the heels of classic gentlemen's shoes, the shoemaker ought to observe the formula of "a quarter the size of the sole plus three-eighths of an inch [1 cm]" to ensure the best possible support. The most commonly found heels are symmetrical and horseshoe shaped. However, there are also asymmetrical heels projecting a little further on the inside than the outside of the shoe, to keep the wearer's foot from turning in.

A heel height of an inch [2.5 cm] is ideal for gentlemen's shoes. It can of course be increased or decreased at the customer's wish, but preferably not by more than three-eighths of an inch [1 cm]. The most comfortable feel in walking is given by a symmetrical heel not set precisely on the center line, and slightly lower on the outside edge. Pointed shoes may have trapezoid heels widening slightly toward the top, while sturdy shoes may have a trapezoid shape widening slightly at the bottom.

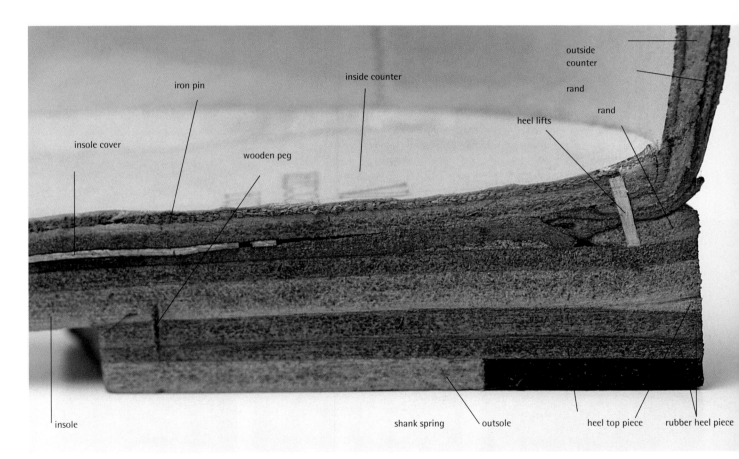

To construct a good, stable heel the shoemaker needs a special feeling for his work, since he will make it out of several layers of leather without using a pattern or model. It takes great skill to make the curve of the heel regular and well adjusted, particularly in view of the fact that the heels of the left and right shoes must match perfectly, and the same applies to the height and thickness of the lifts. Consequently heels are always constructed in pairs.

The heel is made of several "lifts" or layers of leather, about a quarter inch [4–6 mm] thick, built on a second rand that is fixed to the outsole with wooden pegs. The shoemaker compresses the pieces of leather, soaked

in water and kept damp, by hammering them to make the material sturdier, and prevent it from beginning to break up under the constant strain to which it is subjected.

After each lift is fitted, the heel height of both shoes is measured and compared. If the heel of one shoe is too high, then the error is corrected by filing and hammering, and the shoemaker tests the height again.

The last layer on the heel is described by shoemakers as the heel top piece, because it comes into contact with the ground.

The Second Rand

In constructing the heel, the length and the place for the front of the heel are first marked on the shoe in pencil. The height of a heel depends on the size of the shoe: shoes in small sizes have lower heels, shoes in large sizes have higher heels. This ensures greater stability in walking. The shoemaker uses a prepared heel lift as a pattern to establish the size and shape of the heel he is about to make. He files the marked surface smooth, and shaves it with a piece of glass to make it as level as possible. The edges of the heel lift are thinly spread with adhesive to the breadth of the second rand. After the rand is stuck in place, the holes to take the wooden pegs are pre-punched with the awl. The pegs should be long enough to penetrate the sole, the first rand, and the folded edge of the counter, fastening these layers firmly together and giving the heel a stable foundation. Then the surface of the rand is cut with a sharp knife, and the heads of the wooden pegs are filed down to provide as level a surface as possible for the first heel lift. Now the shoe is ready for the construction of the heel, a process described over the next few pages. Yet another fascinating aspect of the shoemaker's craft!

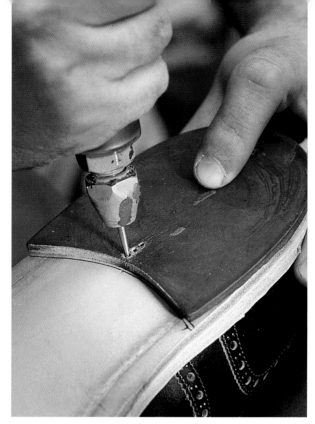

The shoemaker uses a prepared heel lift as a pattern for marking the size of the heel. The three holes mark the place for the front of the heel in different shoe sizes: the first two are for the European shoe sizes 45 and 46, the third is for sizes 39 and 40.

Four to five triangular shapes are cut on the inner edge of the rand, so that the leather strip will fit the curve of the heel.

The shoemaker knocks the wooden pegs into the welt, now glued to the shoe, through holes pre-punched with the awl.

Several layers of leather are cut from the rand with a knife, to make as level as possible a surface for the construction of the heel.

The Construction of the Heel

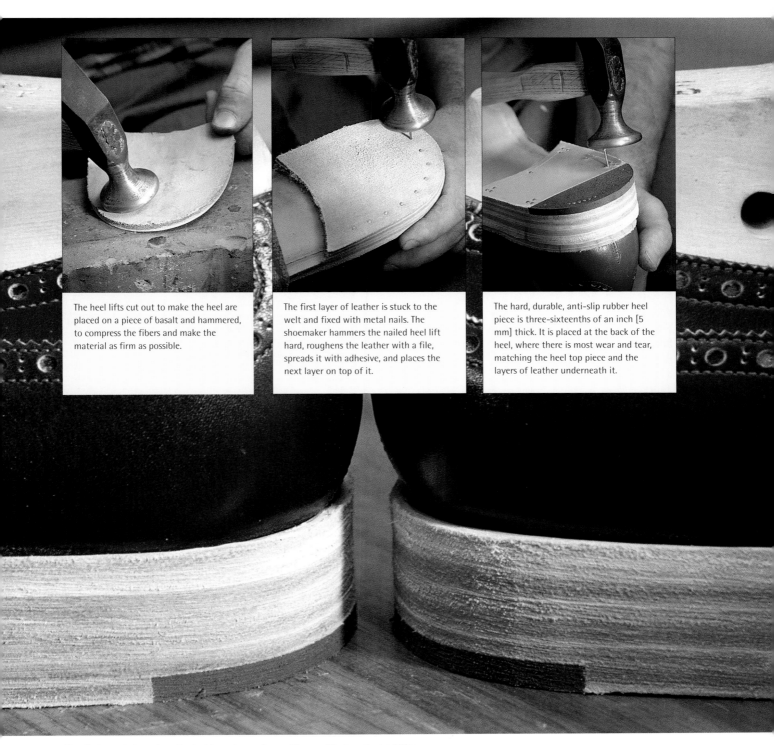

The heel lifts cut out to make the heel are placed on a piece of basalt and hammered, to compress the fibers and make the material as firm as possible.

The first layer of leather is stuck to the welt and fixed with metal nails. The shoemaker hammers the nailed heel lift hard, roughens the leather with a file, spreads it with adhesive, and places the next layer on top of it.

The hard, durable, anti-slip rubber heel piece is three-sixteenths of an inch [5 mm] thick. It is placed at the back of the heel, where there is most wear and tear, matching the heel top piece and the layers of leather underneath it.

The photograph shows how the heel is made up of several layers of leather, the heel lifts.

Measuring and Shaping the Heel

A special feature of the construction of the heel is that it can be done only in pairs, since each layer must be exactly the same height on both heels of a pair of shoes. After each separate lift is fitted, the shoemaker measures them. If the lift turns out too thick in one heel, it is reduced to the size of its counterpart on the other heel by filing and hammering. Once both heels have been constructed the shoemaker finally checks their height again, to make absolutely sure.

Next comes an operation that calls for the greatest care: the shaping of the outside of the heel. The heel is cut to shape all around with a sharp knife, so that the area of the inner ankle forms an angle of 90° with the ground, and the outer part inclines inward from the ground, to keep the foot from wobbling while the wearer of the shoe walks along.

The outside of the heel is hammered to compress and harden the material. The shoemaker keeps damping down the surfaces with a wet brush, and presses the leather edges firmly together with the angular side of the hammer head, striking short blows.

Each time the shoemaker sticks another heel lift in place he trims away the extra material to match the previous lift. In this photograph, only the top heel piece and rubber heel piece still have to be added for the heel to be complete.

Wet leather is softer than dry, so it is easier for the shoemaker to work on the outside of the heel with a knife or hammer if the layers of leather are first moistened with water.

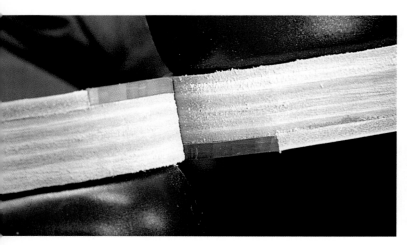

Because of the curve of the counter, the heels can be measured only when the two shoes are set heel to heel.

The damp outside of the heel is hammered and compressed all around, and any traces left by the hammer are removed with a file.

Rubber Heel Pieces

The heel wears most quickly at the place where it first comes into contact with the ground in walking: the outside of the back of the heel. This place can be reinforced with layers of durable material, placed slightly off the central axis of the heel. Hard rubber heel pieces of different shapes are most usual, but burled steel plates are also popular, and it matters little which you prefer for your own shoes.

The most usual shape of heel: symmetrical, with the rubber heel piece slightly longer on the outside.

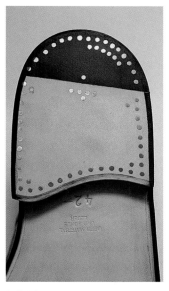

A slightly asymmetrical heel gives particularly good support to flat feet.

Prince William of England, like his father, wears shoes made by Lobb of London – with a rubber heel piece, of course.

The rubber heel piece can come in many different shapes. Here it extends well into the heel top piece.

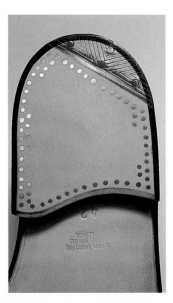

The heel top piece can also be made more durable and less likely to slip with a burled steel plate. This method is very popular in Vienna, although it means that the shoe makes a lot of noise as the wearer walks.

A skiver in the form of a sharp plane with a guide channel in it removes any protruding surfaces of leather, fraction by fraction, matching up the edges of sole and heel.

The shoemaker repeats the same process with a file, forming a curve and compressing the surface.

He runs around the dampened edge of the sole with an edge iron applied cold, exerting strong pressure, to compress the material even more and remove all traces of the file.

Finishing the Sole and Heel

The sole and heel have now been constructed, but work is not yet over: the edge of the sole and the outside of the heel are still a natural leather color, and traces of the shoemaker's work show on their surfaces. The shoemaker now begins the task of "finishing" the shoe, adding embellishments which also help to improve its hardwearing qualities.

If a summer shoe is white or a very light tone (such as pale cognac), the edge of the sole and the outside of the heel are not dyed but remain the natural color of the leather. In other shoes, as a rule, the edges of the sole and heel are dyed the same color as the upper. Black is essential if the upper is black, but any shade is possible with shoes of other colors. However, a shade darker than the upper should always be used. If the edges of the sole and heel are not dyed, the shoemaker simply smooths them with a piece of glass and treats them with colorless or yellowish shoe cream, which is pressed into the leather to make it waterproof. This process emphasizes the natural tone of the leather. A sole treated with shoe cream will be rather slippery at first, but a few steps will roughen up the bottom layer of leather so that it gets a good grip on the ground. If the edges of sole and heel are dyed, the dye must cover the entire bottom of the heel and the outsole in the shank area. A narrow rim about an eighth of an inch [2–3 mm] wide in the appropriate color runs around the outsole. Two ways of dyeing the outsole are most common: in a semi-brogue the shoemaker marks off the dyed area with a straight line echoing the straight toe cap of that type of shoe; in a full brogue with a wing-shaped toe cap the demarcation line is wing shaped too. The attractive finish to the sole of the shoe will last only until the shoes are delivered to the customer and worn for the first time, but the shoemaker is happy to go through a whole series of laborious operations for the sake of this wonderful moment. As with any craft, it is the appreciation of the person who receives the finished item that is most important in the long run, even if by using the item he ultimately will wear it out.

When the hand stitching on the shoe is to be emphasized – as in double-stitched shoes – the shoemaker applies a strongly colored yellow dressing to the stitches and welt. However, the stitches can also be picked out in the same color as the upper or the edge of the sole.

The edges of sole and heel are treated with the desired color. Then a thin layer of wax is applied. The shoemaker presses the color and wax with his anvil and edge iron. The result is a colored surface with a silky gleam.

During the work, irregularities can appear on the surface. These traces are removed with a piece of glass, which shaves away any irregularities by removing fine layers of the sole leather measuring about a hundredth of an inch [0.2–0.4 mm].

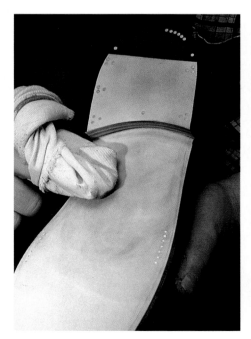

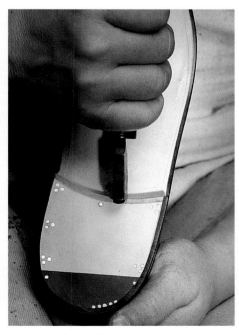

If the outsole and heel top piece are to be natural color, the leather is rubbed several times with colorless shoe cream and allowed to rest for a while, so that the color can sink into the leather as well as possible.

Shoe cream is "melted" into the leather with a heated edge iron.

A very attractive effect is achieved if the shank and the heel top piece are the same color as the edge of the sole.

Ornamentation

Over the years, the way in which the sole and heel are shaped and ornamented has become the trademark of many shoemakers' workshops. These decorative features emphasize the handmade character of the shoe, showing that it is not made by machine, and is very individual. The tool used is called a fancy wheel or crow wheel.

It is used to mark various demarcation lines, for instance at the top of the heel, or on the sole where the dyed and natural surfaces meet. The fancy wheel is heated over a flame to the correct temperature, and the shoemaker rolls it over the surface to be decorated, exerting strong pressure to make sure he achieves the desired effect. The shoe now has a mark of distinction.

The fancy wheel and anvil are heated to the correct temperature over a flame.

This shoe is being decorated with a zigzag pattern at the top and side of the heel.

The edge of the welt of a double-stitched shoe is decorated where it joins the upper with the fancy wheel.

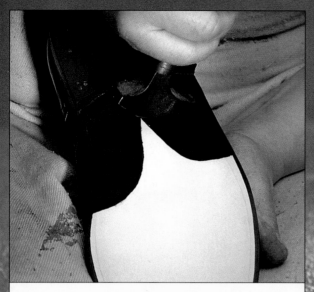

The shank can be decorated with quite an ornamental pattern. The shape shown here is typical of the full-brogue type of shoe, which seems to invite such decoration.

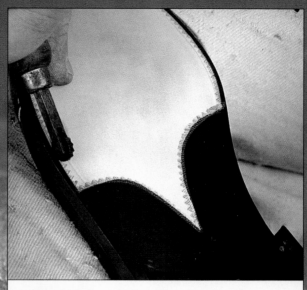

In this model the fancy wheel is being used to add a delicate pattern to the curving demarcation line and the colored line around the outsole.

A historic peculiarity of the shoemaker's craft: the heel of this shoe, which is over fifty years old, was decorated with two different patterns. There are small parallel vertical lines at the top of the side of the heel, and a double row of triangles filled in with dots at a right angle to them. This shows a particular pride in the art of the shoemaker.

Removing the Last

The last has now done its job – the shoe is finished. To complete the final operations, the shoemaker uses his foot-strap and a quarter-inch [6–7 mm] thick iron hook to pull the last carefully out of the shoe, regulating the movement with the foot-strap. The last, once removed, is carefully preserved so that it can be used again to make shoes for the same customer.

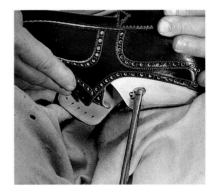

The iron hook is inserted into the hole at the side of the last and tugged slightly with the foot-strap.

The wooden pegs driven into the last through the insole can sit very tightly. Again, the last must be carefully drawn out at this point.

Finishing the Inside of the Shoe

During the various operations involved in shoemaking, wooden pegs can sometimes pierce the interior of the insole, or the metal nails holding the heel lifts together can make holes. If you put a hand inside a shoe from which the last has only just been removed, you may be able to see the ends of nails or feel small bumps. Using special files, the shoemaker smooths over the entire inside surface again. In most cases he provides the whole of the insole with a cover. It is cut from lining leather, with the insole used as a pattern, and must be the same size as the insole. The advantage of a full insole cover is that the whole length of the foot has a soft surface to rest on. The insole cover must be carefully glued in place, or it will work loose while the wearer walks, forming wrinkles which would cause the foot discomfort.

Many customers prefer the foot to come into direct contact with the insole, which has been tanned using vegetable substances, and do not want an insole cover. In that case, the insole is filed first with coarse and then with increasingly fine sandpaper, and buffed to a high gloss. Only a three-quarter or quarter-sized insole cover is added. The overall effect is not so different from a shoe with an insole, and certainly should not be noticeable when walking along.

The insole is filed smooth at the toe with the narrow, long special file, and at the heel with the round file.

If the shoemaker comes upon metal while he is filing the toe of the shoe, there will be a broken nail inside the shoe which must be removed with a pair of pliers.

Insole Covers

Arch Supports

The insole cover, made of the same soft leather as was used for the inside lining of the shoe, is fitted to the smoothed insole. At the customer's wish, it can cover either the whole of the insole, three-quarters of it (from the heel to the ball of the foot), or only a quarter (the heel area).

Many men like shoes with arch supports on which the instep can rest, even though they do not necessarily suffer from sunken plantar arches or flat feet. A shoemaker who knows the measurement of his customer's instep can prepare a cork support and a disk about three-quarters of an inch [2 cm] in diameter, to fit under the instep on the central axis of the ball of the foot.

He inserts these two pieces of cork between the insole and the insole cover – provisionally, for only when the customer tries on the finished shoes and takes a few steps in them will he know if the cork supports are large enough and are in the right place. The shoemaker adjusts them if necessary, making them the right height and length to fit under the arch of the foot, and carefully sticks the insole cover in place.

Medically prescribed supports are not added to the shoe by the shoemaker but placed inside it separately, above the insole cover. The shoemaker will note any information about such supports while he is taking measurements, and will keep them in mind when making the shoe. In such cases the inside of the shoe is usually made a half inch [1 cm] wider than usual, and the upper and counter are cut higher, so that its width can be comfortably adjusted by means of the laces even after the supports are inserted, and the upper and counter will support the foot properly.

Supports added by the shoemaker are not, of course, the same as medically prescribed supports, and merely offer the foot additional comfort.

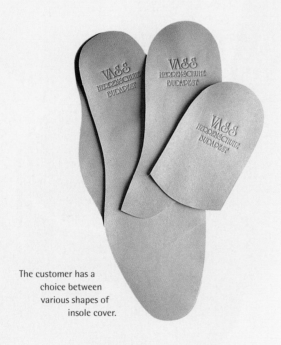

The customer has a choice between various shapes of insole cover.

An insole cover of the desired size is coated with adhesive and stuck inside the shoe.

The cork supports, tapered more thinly at the edges, are inserted between the insole and the insole cover to fit under the arch of the foot.

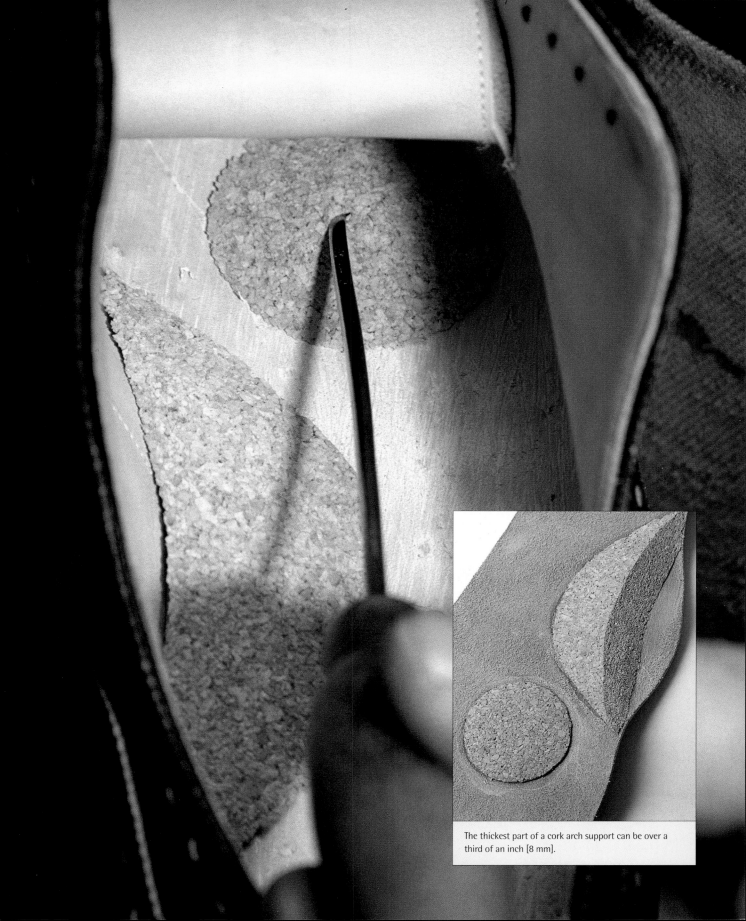

The thickest part of a cork arch support can be over a third of an inch [8 mm].

Shoe Trees

The part played by the shoe tree in the future life of the shoe is as important as the last was in making it. The main task of the shoe tree is to help the shoe retain its original shape as long as possible. For custom-made shoes, the job is best done by custom-made shoe trees matching the original last.

The shoe tree is not exposed to anything like such strains as the last, so different materials can be used to make it. In general, the best material is lightweight wood that can be easily turned on a lathe, and will then present a perfectly smooth surface. The best woods for the purpose are alder (Lat. *Alnus glutinosa*), lime (Lat. *Tilia cordata*), cedar (Lat. *Cedrus*), and cherry (Lat. *Prunus*); the last-named is a popular choice because of its attractive grain.

The felled timber is prepared in the same way and with as much careful attention as the wood for lasts. Up to a point, the operations of making a shoe tree and making a last are so similar that at first glance you cannot tell which is going on.

The final operations in the making of lasts and shoe trees, however, are very different: a shoe tree turned from a block of wood must be easy to insert into the shoe and to remove again. The two most usual and popular types of shoe trees are three-part shoe trees and sprung shoe trees (see page 188).

The natural materials of leather and wood go very well together, and provide a link to the past which is most appreciated by many shoemakers.

Carefully prepared blocks of wood, already suggesting the shape of a shoe tree, await further working to become custom-made shoe trees.

The custom-made last is placed on the lathe and its shape registered by sensors, so that the shape of the shoe tree can reflect it.

One of the favorite materials for shoe trees is alder, from a tree that, when grown in moist areas with plenty of water, forms a trunk 16 inches [40 cm] in diameter within the comparatively short period of 30–40 years.

The Three-part Shoe Tree

The shoe tree is sawn into two parts in front of the knob, with the wood held slightly on the slant.

The same operation is performed behind the knob at the heel; the shoe tree is now in three parts.

The toe of the shoe tree is inserted into the shoe first, and then the heel. The wedge-shaped central section with the knob on it is pushed firmly between the two parts and thus stretches the shoe.

The Sprung Shoe Tree

The shoe tree is sawn into three, but the central part is taken right out.

The components of the sprung shoe tree are the heel, the butt, the spring, the pin, and the front. They are fitted together and fixed in place.

The completed shoe tree is rubbed with a thin coating of beeswax and polished to a high gloss with a soft cloth.

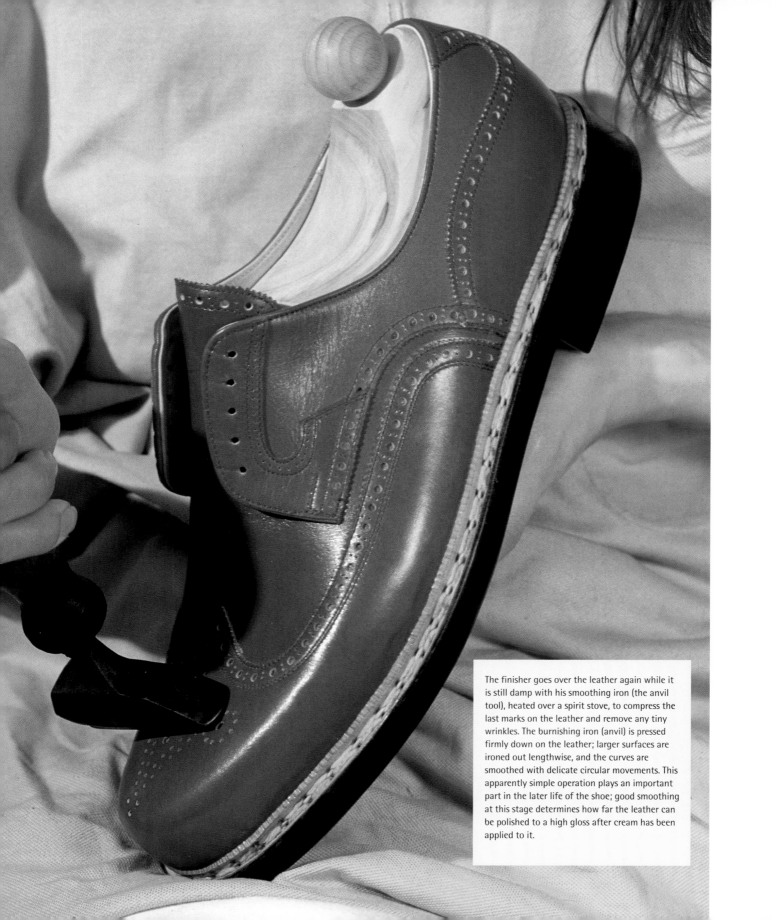

The finisher goes over the leather again while it is still damp with his smoothing iron (the anvil tool), heated over a spirit stove, to compress the last marks on the leather and remove any tiny wrinkles. The burnishing iron (anvil) is pressed firmly down on the leather; larger surfaces are ironed out lengthwise, and the curves are smoothed with delicate circular movements. This apparently simple operation plays an important part in the later life of the shoe; good smoothing at this stage determines how far the leather can be polished to a high gloss after cream has been applied to it.

Finishing the Completed Shoe

Now only the final delicate operations remain. In the hands of the finisher, the upper reveals itself as a work of art. However carefully we tend our shoes at home, they will never shine exactly as they did at the moment of purchase. The finisher may use the same creams and cloths or brushes, but will achieve a better result, perhaps because of his experience. One small comfort is that the customer can take his shoes back to the workshop where they were created to be cleaned at any time!

Any remains of adhesive and fingerprints left by the shoemaker are removed from the upper with lukewarm soapy water. However much trouble the master craftsman has taken, it is inevitable that the glue on his fingers will leave marks behind on the upper.

Attention must be paid to the smallest details in the operations of smoothing, applying shoe cream, and polishing the upper. For instance, in shoes of the full-brogue type, the leather under the edges of the ornamental holes is lighter than the dyed surface and must be colored at a later stage. The bristles of a toothbrush will work the shoe cream into the smallest interstices.

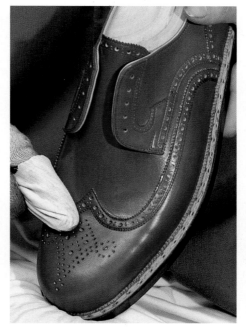

The gloss on the shoe depends on how well the areas between marks invisible to the naked eye are filled in. Once the surface has been compressed by ironing, the finisher removes the tiny differences that still remain with shoe cream. He uses a soft cloth soaked in shoe cream and wrapped around his finger, describing circular movements and applying light pressure, thus creating an almost mirrorlike surface. The secret of this glossy surface is to apply the cream to the leather in a thin layer and leave it to soak in for at least 15 minutes, repeating the process three or four times. Finally, the finisher uses a soft brush and flannel cloth to buff the shoe to a high gloss.

Every famous shoemaking workshop takes a pride in its products and gives them its own trademark. This can be the name of the workshop, or an easily identifiable logo, or some indirect indication, perhaps the way in which the sole of the shoe is colored, or the design of the heel top piece. The direct method is the most effective. For instance, the firm's logo may appear on the insole cover, and also on the shoe tree, as a small copper plate bearing the firm's logo (the example here is from the Vass workshop in Budapest).

The typical lacing of Oxfords, a procedure that all true gentlemen will follow.

The typical lacing of Derbys, contrasting with Oxfords.

Suitable Shoelaces

Fabric laces are best for made-to-measure gentlemen's shoes: round laces will suit elegant shoes, and either round or ribbon laces look good with sturdy shoes. Both kinds of lace are made by machine. Round laces are cylindrical, with a core made of cotton waste or hemp yarn. Ribbon laces usually have no core. To facilitate the threading of the laces through the eyelets, the ends have cylindrical metal tags fitted.

The color of the shoelace must always suit the color of the upper; at most it may be a shade darker, but certainly no lighter. If the upper of the shoe is in a combination of colors, then the laces should match the darker color. Their length depends on the number of eyelets: for shoes with five to six eyelets, the ideal length of the laces is about 30 inches [75 cm]; for shoes with up to four eyelets it is 2 feet [60 cm]. In this way a bow of the right size can be tied when the laces have been threaded through. Boots need laces 4 feet [120 cm] long.

Both Oxfords and Derbys have their characteristic styles of lacing, but it can be varied as you like. The methods are no longer bound to the original model. However, tradition will always play a part, and most wearers will prefer to lace their shoes in the usual way for a particular style. Many people will recognise this care for what is customary as the mark of a gentleman.

Packing material has only a temporary function, to protect the shoe until it is handed over to the customer. However, the fabric bag should be kept, since the shoes will be better kept in it than in a shoe rack or shoe box. The bag keeps dust off, and has no hard surfaces against which the shoe might rub, as a shoe box does.

Packing

Packing the shoes can help to protect them until the customer receives them, and the packaging will act as somewhere to keep them for any length of time. Shoes should generally be kept in the dark anyway, since light has a harmful effect on leather in the long run. It is a good idea to protect the two shoes of a pair separately. A small bag of soft flannel, linen, or cashmere in which the shoe is placed is suitable; the bag can be closed with a drawstring, and will protect the shoe from dust or from any damage to its upper done by the edge of the sole of the other shoe. The shoes can be stored either upright, or on their sides in a shoe box of suitable size. This may all seem an excessive form of protection, but the shoes will certainly benefit, as will their owner.

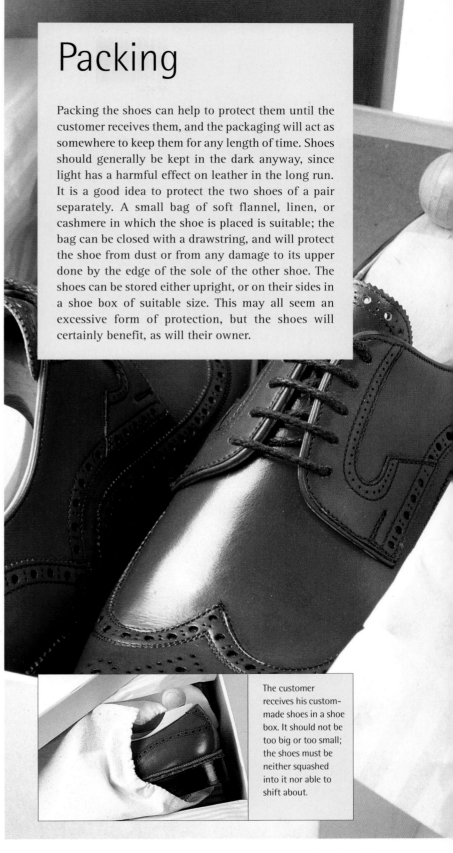

The customer receives his custom-made shoes in a shoe box. It should not be too big or too small; the shoes must be neither squashed into it nor able to shift about.

Caring for Shoes

Cleaning

Only meticulous care enables the upper leather of a shoe to retain its suppleness, its resilience, and its attractive gleam. At the same time clean, well-cared-for shoes always make their wearer look very well dressed. If footwear is not looked after, its leather, sooner or later, will become brittle – particularly where it bends – and crack. Uncared-for shoes inevitably have a relatively short life expectancy.

The meticulous care of his shoes becomes a pleasant routine task for the owner, as long as he possesses a fully-equipped shoe-care kit. If it includes all the necessary utensils, all he has to do is make sure the work is carried out in the correct order.

The kit should contain at least one cleaning brush made of pig bristles or the tailhair of cattle or horses; also popular are brushes made of agave fibers, the tough, flexible leaf fibers of a South American species of agave. Dried-on mud and the like is removed by the stiff bristles of these dense brushes.

You need one putting-on brush, generally consisting of soft horsehair, for each different color of shoe you own. Using a single brush to put on different-colored polishes should be avoided, as the dried residues may mix together, leading to uneven coloring and even different shades. Shoes consisting of leather of more than one color complicate the cleaning process. If your collection of shoes includes a pair of Spectators, for example, you will need two brushes for them alone: a black one for the black leather, a white one for the white. If need be, the putting-on brushes can be replaced by toothbrushes or by white cloths.

The number of polishes, creams, and liquids should be the same as the number of putting-on brushes. If you have first-class shoes it obviously makes sense to use first-class cleansing agents that exactly match the color of the leather – unless you want to give your shoes an "antique" look as quickly as possible, in which case it is advisable to use shoe creams a few shades darker: dark-claret cream on light-claret leather, light or dark-brown cream on light cognac, black on brown. A thin layer of the cleansing agent is applied to the leather and left to penetrate it for at least ten minutes.

The shoe-care kit must also contain taking-off brushes, which are generally made of hair from horses' manes or tails. Again, several may be needed, depending on the number of colors. Once the cream has been applied and left to be absorbed, these are used to polish up the shoes to a high gloss. A white cloth can again be substituted for the taking-off brush, and indeed where shoes have very thin leather it is most advisable to polish them exclusively with cloths because of the danger of erosion. This danger should not be underestimated, because leather is very susceptible to such damage, which will shorten the life of shoes.

Every owner of handmade shoes should possess a shoe-care kit carefully chosen on the basis of their color. Best results are obtained by using a shoe cream one shade darker than the color of the shoes. Light-colored summer footwear is cleaned with colorless shoe cream. The latter is often described as "neutral."

The Ten Golden Rules of Shoe Care

When he ceremonially hands over a new pair of shoes to their owner, at the moment when a unique work of art passes from artist to purchaser, the shoemaker also initiates him into the secrets of shoe care. The life expectancy and appearance of new custom-made shoes depends on the quality of the material used and the expertise of the shoemaker, certainly, but they also depend to a great extent on the care they receive from their wearer. Trying the shoes on and walking in them for a few minutes will tell the customer whether they fit or not. If these qualities are to be preserved over an extended period, it is advisable to follow a few "golden rules":

1. New shoes should initially be worn for no more than two or three hours at a time. Only when the shoes and the feet are completely accustomed to each other should the risk be taken of wearing them for a whole day.

2. A pair of shoes should not be worn on two successive days, but should be given 24 hours to recover after each wearing.

3. They should always be put on with a shoehorn, regardless of whether they are lace-ups, buckled shoes, or slip-ons.

4. When taking off lace-up shoes the laces should first be loosened at every point, allowing the foot to slip out of the shoe easily and effortlessly.

5. Custom-made shoe trees must be inserted in the shoes immediately after removal.

6. Shoe trees should be inserted immediately even if the shoes have been saturated with rain or snow. The shoes should then be left to dry, lying on their sides rather than standing on their soles, for at least 24 hours.

7. It is advisable to wipe the shoes down and polish them up with shoe cream after each wearing, even if they appear to have lost none of their original gleam.

8. If the shoes are not to be worn for an extended period, a thin coating of cream should be applied, a textile bag obtained from the shoemaker, and the shoes placed inside it in their original box, standing on their soles.

9. No owner of custom-made shoes should lend them to somebody else, for no two pairs of feet are the same.

10. Every new shoe has its own special character: its true beauty will not appear to its best advantage unless it is worn with appropriate clothing and on appropriate occasions.

The Art of Shoe Cleaning

Around the turn of the century shoe cleaning developed into a fully fledged profession in the United States of America. The "Shoe Shine Service," shoe cleaning in the street, still has a certain magic about it today: many a shoe cleaner on Wall Street, New York, has been there so long that he has become part of the scenery, and his customers are devoted to him. As professional shoe cleaners they are intimately familiar with all the tricks of the trade, learned over many years.

Shoe cleaning is a lengthy business. Even the tiniest speck of dirt must be carefully brushed away, for the purpose of applying the cream is not to get rid of residual dirt but rather to replenish the leather with the substances – grease, wax, and moisture – that it loses in wear.

The shoe cleaner applies the cream with slow, circular movements, putting on exactly as much as the leather needs. If the leather is very dehydrated the shoe cleaner lets the first layer of shoe cream penetrate it before applying the next. A thick layer of cream is hardly absorbed at all, and afterward the leather is extremely difficult to polish.

Whether the polishing is done with a brush or a cloth, the main thing is to make sure that the equipment is always spotlessly clean.

Looking after full-brogues is a particularly intense and time-consuming activity because they have opulent perforations. When cream gets into the holes, brushing must continue until the most minuscule residue has been removed. Any shoe cream that is left in the holes will instantly attract the dust. And however richly the shoes gleam after polishing, they will still look neglected.

Today's shoe creams are equal to the most exacting requirements. But one old trick still works: moistening the shoes with saliva now and again while cleaning them. This has both a cleansing and a polishing effect, and is especially useful in emergencies.

The shoe to be cleaned is placed on this stand.

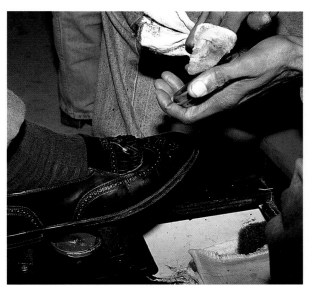

Shoe cream must get into every hole of a full-brogue.

Cream must also be applied to the rim of the sole and the heel.

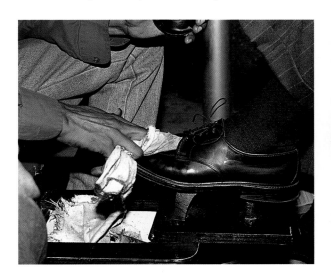

Superfluous shoe cream must be wiped away.

The toe cap is cleaned with horizontal movements.

Types of Shoe Tree

The three-piece shoe trees made to go with custom-made shoes, which are also called hinged shoe trees, are an important element in shoe care. Sooner or later shoes stored without shoe trees lose their shape, and the leather develops creases and breaks. Shoes exposed to above-average volumes of perspiration lose their shape extraordinarily quickly if stored without shoe trees. Also shoes are easier to look after and clean if they are kept on trees, because their leather retains its vigor and smoothness for a longer period.

There is a widespread view that after being worn shoes must "cool off" before the shoe trees are inserted. In fact it is advisable to insert the shoe trees immediately after taking them off, while they are still warm; this smoothes out any creases, and their original attractive shape is retained until the next time they are worn.

Custom-made shoe trees belong exclusively to the shoes for which they were originally made. On no account may they be used with other shoes, for their shapes would not coincide.

The three-piece shoe trees, even though they are made of light wood, are the heaviest. This is why many wearers prefer the light, sprung shoe trees with removable centers. The so-called hinged shoe trees, or those with a handle and adjustable screw, weigh even less.

Shoe trees do not require any special care, but even so they should be wiped with a damp cloth every three months.

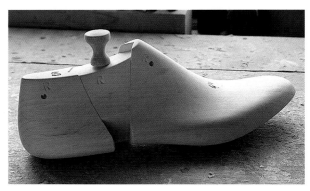

The classic shoe tree has a simple, three-piece design.

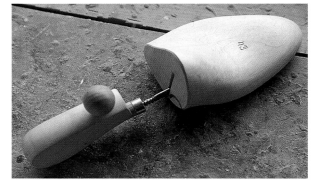

The superfluous wood has been removed from the front and rear of the sprung shoe tree.

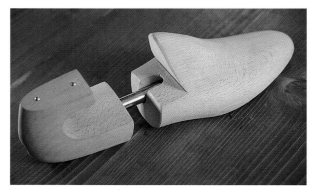

The shoe tree with a handle and adjustable screw is effective at the front of the shoe, but ineffective at the heel cup. It is most suitable for traveling, although it can also be used at home.

This elegantly shaped hinged shoe tree in a matching color has a simple hinge, making it easy to open and close.

The Shoe Horn

If any shoe is put on without a shoe horn, its heel buckles, stretches, and cracks. When selecting a shoe horn – regardless of whether it is of metal, wood, or actual horn – you should ensure that it has a totally smooth surface and does not break under strain.

When inserted into the shoe, the shoe horn forms a sort of guide rail that covers and stiffens the heel cup while the foot slides in. If the shoe is still new, its upper may "give" very little – and it may not be easy to put on even with the assistance of a shoe horn. In this event the wearer should carefully work his foot into the shoe with a series of small movements.

If no shoe horn is to hand, your two index fingers make a good substitute – though in the long term this does neither the fingers nor the heel cup any good. A handkerchief is more effective: it is placed inside the shoe against the heel cup and the heel slid into the shoe, the

Shoe horns made of real horn (shown here in various lengths) are particularly flexible and comfortable.

Even the simple metal shoe horn serves its purpose.

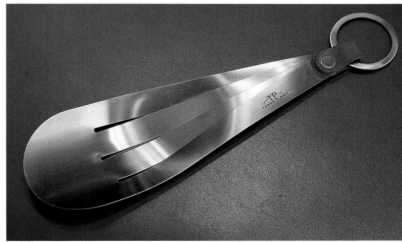
A particularly attractive design in metal with a hollow that follows the contours of the heel.

handkerchief being simultaneously removed.

A long shoe horn should be used to put on ankle boots; naturally it can also be used with ordinary shoes, and so it may be sensible to buy this type of shoe horn, as you will not need any other.

A shoe horn is clearly as important an item in any gentleman's shoe care equipment as any other, and care should be taken in selecting the right one.

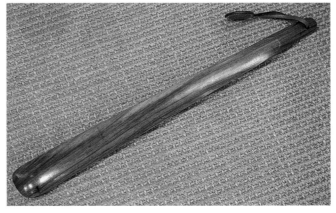
The longer shoe horn is used with both boots and shoes.

"If the Shoe Pinches..."

The width of the upper can also be increased by up to a quarter inch [0.5 cm] with a metal stretcher, the front part of which is opened with a screw. As a rule a minute or two is sufficient, but, depending on the thickness of the upper leather, a shoe may have to be stretched for anything up to 24 hours.

The shoemaker inserts the front part of the stretcher in the shoe, moistens the upper leather, and stretches the shoe by slowly turning the screw. This avoids bursting the stitches and tearing the leather.

Manual stretching is carried out with a screwed shoe tree – actually the front part of a last sawn in two – that is inserted in the shoe. As with the stretcher, the shoemaker increases the distance between the two halves by turning the screw. The advantage of this is that the shoemaker holds the shoe in his hand throughout the process and thus has a better idea of how much it needs to be stretched.

When the process is finished, a cork filler between one-eighth and one-twelfth of an inch [2 or 3 mm] thick is placed inside the shoe beneath the inner sole. Often it is sufficient to place a partial filler in the front part of the shoe. In addition the wearer can regulate the width of the upper with the laces. If the upper edge is too close to the ankle, the shoemaker inserts a cork filler up to one-fifth of an inch [5 mm] thick in the heel.

Shoes are always repaired in pairs. Even if only one of them has a hole in the sole, the shoemaker always resoles both – in order to avoid maintenance discrepancies between the two. The tools used are the same ones used to make them in the first place.

Shoe Repairs

Handsewn classic shoes never go out of fashion. If they are made with care and properly looked after, they can be worn for several decades – and the more they are worn, the more refined they become. The owner of a good pair of shoes is often more fond of them after wearing them for years than he was when they were new: he has grown accustomed to them, they have become a part of him, and he cannot do without them.

After a long time, however, even the most perfect shoes begin to wear out. When this happens depends on the weight and bearing of the wearer, how often they are

worn, and how well they are looked after. Wear is most often found on the heels and the soles, and the toe caps are commonly damaged. In these cases the shoes should be returned for repair to the workshop where they were made, which will carry out the work in the interests of good customer relations.

There are only two cases in which it is necessary to bid farewell to a favorite pair of shoes: if the heel cups have buckled or either the leather or seams of the uppers have ruptured so badly that repairs are not possible. In such cases, one has to bow to the inevitable.

Repairs to the Toe Piece and the Heel

After long use the first parts of the shoe to show signs of wear are the toe piece and the heel. The thickness of the sole leather may vary by up to one-eighth of an inch [3 mm] as a result of heavy wear. Care should be taken that the welt stitching in the channel is not damaged. Restoring the sole to its original thickness is a relatively simple repair.

The shoemaker cleans the attached piece of leather with a rasp, a fragment of broken glass, and with coarse and fine sandpaper until both the edges of the sole and the join between the old and new parts are as smooth as possible.

The shoemaker cuts into the sole 2 inches [5 cm] from the toe piece and removes the worn leather, in tiny fractions of an inch at a time, with a sharp knife – taking care not to damage the seam. Then he cuts a piece of tough leather to fit, sticks it on with adhesive, and secures it with wood pegs, ready for smoothing down.

Even though a particularly tough quarter rubber is generally incorporated in the back of the heel, this is the first part to show wear – for it is placed under maximum strain with every step the wearer takes. If only the rubber is affected, replacing it is similar to the process carried out on the sole.

If the top heel is damaged, however, the shoemaker must remove the worn leather, the quarter rubber, and the leather underneath it, then rebuild the heel, almost from scratch.

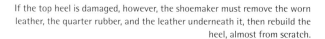

Replacing the Sole and Heel

If the sole is heavily worn – and particularly if there is an actual hole in it – more extensive repairs are necessary, though if a shoe has a double sole these can be kept within acceptable limits; as long as the sole seams and middle sole are undamaged, all that is required is a half-sole – a sort of extended toe piece. The shoemaker removes the worn part of the sole as far as the waist with a knife, being careful to avoid damaging the seams, then fits a new sole.

Sometimes, because of the wearer's unusual gait, wear is concentrated not on the center of the sole but on its outer or inner edges. This wear may be so heavy that it even damages the sole seam, loosening the stitches and perhaps destabilizing the welt. In this event the repair has two main stages: the custom-made last is inserted into the shoe, which the shoemaker dismantles to its very base

(the welt) and then rebuilds. If this sort of "general overhaul" is being carried out, it makes sense to replace the welt itself. The resulting gap is filled, the new sole sewn onto the welt, and the heel rebuilt.

One question will inevitably be asked: whether it is worth carrying out such extensive repairs; but experience has shown that a comfortable pair of shoes, already adapted to the shape of its owner's feet, is virtually irreplaceable, and that major or minor repairs represent a sort of rebirth. Many customers of master shoemakers are delighted to find that their favorite shoes are not destined for the scrapheap, and are in fact capable of repair and many more years of pleasure. This is a major advantage with custom-made shoes.

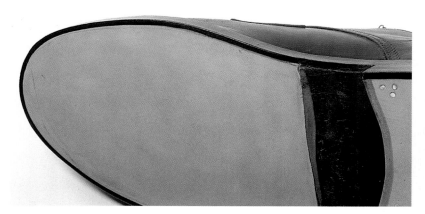

Though the sole has a hole in it, the seams are undamaged – so all that is required is a new half-sole – a great relief to the customer!

With new soles and heels, the old shoes begin a new life.

If the seam is worn or damaged, it is advisable to replace the welt too.

Workshops

Shoes Fit for a King:
Lobb in London and Paris

The founder of the workshop in London's St. James's Street, John Lobb, the son of a farmer, was born at Tywardreath in Cornwall in 1829. His masterly command of the craft earned him major prizes at international exhibitions during the Victorian period. In 1863 Lobb became the proud holder of a Royal Warrant, which identified him as Prince Edward's bootmaker. The name of the future King Edward VII (1841-1910) still conjures up an era in which Lobb's shoes were a byword for the utmost elegance and quality. The example given by the prince was copied by the rich and famous in England and elsewhere, including kings, nawabs, and maharajas (Muslim and Hindu rulers in India); actors, opera singers, politicians, and writers. Opera fans might visit Lobb in the hope of meeting Enrico Caruso, Feodor Chalyapin, or John McCormack; business people might have the opportunity to pick up tips there from Andrew Carnegie, Bernard Oppenheimer, or Guglielmo Marconi; while budding writers could admire George Bernard Shaw or even the man who gave his name to the most important literary prize in the world, Joseph Pulitzer himself.

For well over 100 years Lobb have survived all the social changes and financial ups and downs of business life to which the traditional shoemakers in the West End of London are particularly exposed. In all this time the company has maintained the tradition of craftsmanship for which it has been renowned among generations of shoemakers and customers who wish to follow in the footsteps of the famous.

As long as there are demanding customers who truly appreciate the outstanding comfort and quality of these unique bespoke shoes made of the best leather and designed to fit each wearer's foot individually, Lobb enterprise will endure.

This family firm continues to hold the unique triple Royal Warrant that marks out Lobb as bootmaker to Her Majesty Queen Elizabeth II, His Royal Highness the Duke of Edinburgh, and His Royal Highness the Prince of Wales. The Lobb tradition is still very much alive and flourishes to the present day.

John Lobb continues to flourish because the firm has recognized the need to provide a high-quality service to its customers, while appreciating changing fashions and the durability of classic designs, which the true gentleman will always require.

In 1901, at a time when many traditional shoemakers were being forced to shut down as the rapidly expanding shoe industry swamped the market with cheap, fashionable shoes, Lobb were opening a branch in Paris. This shop introduced English traditions of shop fitting, customer service, and quality footwear to the French "metropolis."

In the shadow of the great gate of St. James's Palace in London, the royal residence from 1699 to 1837, you will find No. 9 St. James's Street, where the English poet Lord Byron (1788-1824) lived as a young bachelor. The building now houses the premises of the bootmakers John Lobb. The three Royal Warrants above the door instantly identify the firm as a supplier to the Royal Family. With its coffee shops, gentlemen's clubs, and elegant fashion houses, St. James's Street has been a place of pilgrimage for cultivated, fashion-conscious gentlemen from London and beyond for hundreds of years.

"The most beautiful shoe shop in the world," as the English magazine *Esquire* described the elegant, wood-paneled premises of John Lobb. The London shop displays shoes from Lobb's Paris collection in a case.

London and Budapest Meet: Benjamin Klemann in Basthorst

Benjamin Klemann was born in 1959 on the North-Sea island of Föhr. Since 1990 he has been running a bespoke shoemaker's in a small workshop on the idyllic Basthorst estate to the east of Hamburg. From a young age Klemann nursed an ambition to become a shoemaker. Working his way up from the bottom, he was taken on in Neumünster by the Hungarian Julius Harai, from whom he learned the craft of the bespoke shoemaker. A name known beyond the circles of shoe-industry insiders, Harai trained Klemann in the traditions of Hungarian shoemaking. After completing his apprenticeship, Klemann perfected his skills further and went to England in 1986, where he worked on a freelance basis for the Royal-Warrant holders Lobb. In London Klemann was also employed by Foster and Son, New and Lingwood, and Alan McAfee. This experience gave him the opportunity to learn the art of making elegant British shoes.

Together with his wife, Magrit, who is a master closer, Klemann has been training apprentices for several years. He places great emphasis on the fact that all the work undertaken in his workshop is carried out under his own personal supervision.

This selection of shoes proves Klemann to be a master of the two classic schools of shoemaking. There is a particular beauty to the shoes in which he has brought together English elegance and Hungarian style. Above all else Klemann prizes the finest box calf and kidskin, but also uses exotic leathers such as ostrich, shark, crocodile, and kangaroo. As far as Klemann is concerned, tradition and experimentation go hand in hand; he has even created perfect full-brogue shoes with leather recovered from a ship that sank off Plymouth 200 years ago (see page 88). There seems no doubt that he enjoys a challenge!

Form follows function: Himer & Himer in Baden-Baden

The youngest of the traditional bespoke shoemakers in Europe, Axel Himer, born in 1965, decided he wanted to be a shoemaker when he visited the workshop of an orthopedic shoemaker he knew. It might be possible, he mused, to make orthopedic shoes that were more beautiful and distinguished than the conventional products. "But there's no market for that," his friend told him gloomily. "We'll see about that," Axel Himer said to himself, and set about achieving his aim.

His solid training in Cologne, Stuttgart, Hanover, and Heidelberg and his work as an orthopedic shoemaker stand him in good stead today. His comprehensive knowledge of anatomy and broad understanding of technical questions make his work easier and help him to solve even the most intractable cases.

Himer's work is unmistakable: the best leather and other selected materials are used to make wonderfully comfortable, perfectly fitting shoes. Axel Himer has added one extra procedure to the usual steps when taking measurements (see pages 12 ff.): he makes foam casts of the customer's feet. Among other things, this enables him to produce a perfect footbed. He believes that trial shoes are only worthwhile if they are made of real leather and the customer wears them for at least 14 days. If there are still problems after this time, the shoemaker will make the necessary corrections on the last. Himer & Himer are also known for their golf shoes; after all, people are not just right-handed or left-handed, but right-footed and left-footed as well since their feet are asymmetric and bear different amounts of load. Himer golf shoes are built to take account of these personal idiosyncrasies.

For Axel Himer the greatest challenge facing a shoemaker is that of helping people who have difficulties with their feet and making beautiful shoes that allow them to walk without pain.

The maxim "form follows function" has made this small shop famous. Our feet carry our whole weight, so our shoes need to fit perfectly. Axel Himer and his wife Christine place great emphasis on comfort and adherence to orthopedic principles.

The Baldessarini/Hugo Boss collection created in the workshop of László Vass combines 100 years of tradition with modern design. The shoes displayed at his suitably elegant premises provide points of reference for his demanding customers as they select the footwear they desire for whatever occasion.

A Budapest Renaissance: László Vass

László Vass, born in Budapest in 1946, belongs to a generation of shoemakers who were brave and energetic enough to go back to the roots of their craft and revive a rich, old tradition, giving the art of shoemaking new impetus in a new age.

The skills of the master shoemakers who lived and worked in Budapest on the banks of the Danube at the beginning of the twentieth century reached their apogee in the shoe that was named, in their honor, after the city. The Budapest, a full-brogue Derby with a high toe cap, was famous and popular under this name in London, Paris, New York, and Rome.

In 1970 Vass passed a special shoemaker's exam in which he had to make a pair of hand-sewn Budapests. Since then he has set himself the aim of making Budapests that attain the very highest standards. László Vass's shop is situated in the very heart of Budapest at No. 2 Haris Köz. It is practically a place of pilgrimage; his customers come from all corners of Europe to order hand-sewn shoes of supreme quality. His revival of Hungarian bespoke shoemaking has been recognised with one of Hungary's greatest state honors.

After working for five years at the Hungarian fashion house Magyar Divatintézet as a clicker, closer, shoemaker, and designer, Vass knew all the secrets of shoemaking. The objective of all his work is to make bespoke shoes in various styles, shapes, and colors that are as comfortable, elegant, and long lasting as possible.

The Name is a Brand:
Bálint in Vienna

A Hungarian from Transylvania by birth, the 45-year-old Lajos Bálint began a new life as an unknown craftsman when he moved to Vienna with his wife Kati. Within a decade he had transformed his name into a brand. Bálint has become famous for his precision when taking measurements and the perfection of the lasts he makes. He sees good shoes as a sign of confidence and health consciousness, as important as any other consideration of one's well-being.

Bálint's remarkable bespoke shoes are the fruit of centuries of tradition. They are real classics, and demand a perfect outfit to go with them, an outfit that is suitably complementary to their style.

Style, Success, and Quality:
Materna in Vienna

The proprietor of the wonderful shop in the shadow of the world-famous Vienna Opera House, the 59-year-old Georg Materna, is the king of the Viennese shoemakers. Like a doctor reading an X-ray, he is able to absorb all the information he needs for his work from a customer's footprints and the measurements taken when a pair of shoes is ordered. High-quality materials and immaculate craftsmanship are united inseparably in a Materna shoe. This is why his customers are more than ready to wait six to eight weeks for their shoes. The philosophy of Materna's workshop is that expensive shoes are good business - not just for the shoemaker, but also for the customer. Someone who looks after his shoes properly will still enjoy their comfort and elegance 20 years after he bought them. The craft is a tradition in Materna's family. His father and grandfather were both shoemakers, and even the grandchildren of their customers have yet to wear out the Materna shoes purchased by earlier generations.

Visitors to Vienna are able to marvel at the impressive selection of Materna designs in his shop window, including welted and lock-stitched shoes, Oxfords, Derbys, Monks, slippers, boots, and golf shoes.

Four Generations of Outstanding Quality: Berluti in Paris

Alessandro Berluti (1865-1922) was born in Senigallia, a village near Urbino in Italy. Thanks to his skill as a leather worker, the shoes he made soon found great acclaim. Loaded with his old shoemaking equipment, he went to Paris in 1887. To the present day the house of Berluti faithfully upholds the art of making bespoke shoes that was so commonly practiced during his lifetime.

Berluti's son Torello (1885-1959) created the famous Berluti spirit, which gained him customers like James de Rothschild, Sacha Distel, Bernard Blier, and Yul Brynner. He found an ideal location for his shop at rue Marbeuf No. 26. Between 1960 and 1980 Torello's son Talbinio expanded the company, which won ever more international plaudits. At the end of his life he left everything to his cousin Olga.

The Berluti collection reflects the aesthetic values that Olga Berluti stands for. Her approach is summed up by the question: How do I make shoes that incarnate the qualities of classical beauty, the lyrical, the well made, the exquisite? Olga Berluti has been able to resolve this question time and again thanks to her superb mastery of patina, which makes it possible for her to create unprecedented color effects. She joined the family firm in 1959, and ten years later her style in form and coloring had become the Berluti visiting card.

The "piazza," one of the four rooms at the Berluti shop, along with the "salon," the "lounge," and the "grotto." The room looks like a shrine: marble from Carrara, solar motifs, wrought-iron arabesques, and stained-glass chandeliers serve as a background for the shoes on display. A selection of shoes in unusual shades and shapes is arranged in a semicircle and holds the viewer spellbound with its forms and colors. Olga Boluti's color mastery is at the heart of this, giving the display aesthetic brilliance.

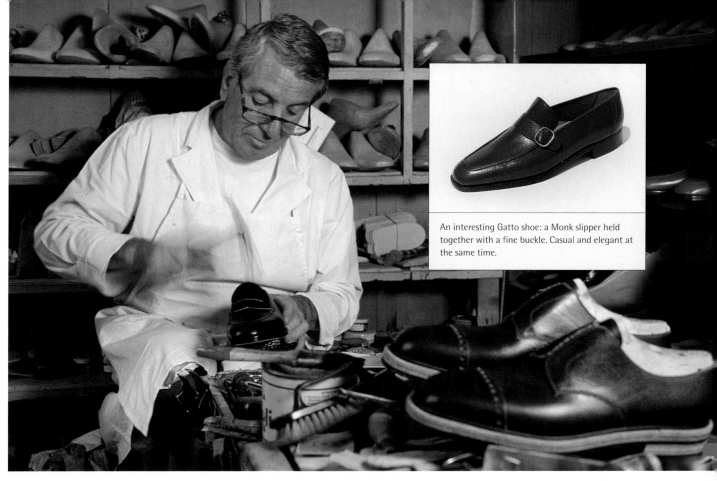

An interesting Gatto shoe: a Monk slipper held together with a fine buckle. Casual and elegant at the same time.

Gatto shoes look so timeless that they give us an awareness of eternity. "Most of our customers - many of them of noble origin - stay with us for decades," says Vincenzo Gatto, the current owner of the business.

Another Wonder of Rome: Gatto

There is no shop window and no neon lighting to indicate the presence of one of the most famous shoemaking workshops in Europe at No. 34 Via Salandra in Rome; just a simple sign bearing the words "Gatto 1st Story." An article published by the German magazine *Stern* in 1988 quoted one of Gatto's many famous customers, King Alfonso XIII of Spain, who once praised the small workshop in the following words: "There are two wonders in Rome: the Sistine Chapel and Gatto's shoes." The business was founded in 1912 by Angelo Gatto and has been welcoming famous customers at its premises since the 1930s - including princes, kings, diplomats, industrialists, and stars of film and music, such as Tony Curtis, Maurice Chevalier, and Paul Anka.

A full-brogue Oxford from the Gatto workshop. Most Italian shoes are long and narrow. This shoe, with its decorated seams on the upper, is a real classic of the style.

A Commitment to Quality: E. Vogel in New York

E. Vogel have been in family ownership since 1879. They are firmly committed to the principle of fitting their customers out with the best shoes possible. E. Vogel's bespoke shoes are designed to be perfectly balanced and highly comfortable so that the owner's feet move easily when walking. Attention to the slightest of details and extraordinary durability are the hallmarks of this workshop.

For a long time Dean Vogel, Egidius's great-grandson and the current manager, made riding boots for the USA's Olympic team, as well as for other prominent equestrians. "I have had customers," he says, "who ordered boots from us for years on end before they noticed that we had shoes in our collection. When they asked how long we had been making shoes, I would say: 'Oh, for about 120 years!'"

Surrounded by cheap Chinese restaurants and sweet shops, No. 19 Howard Street is a unique building. The cellar houses an archive containing more than 1600 handmade lasts. The card index reads like a who's who of historic personalities, including General Pershing, Charles Lindbergh, and Paul Newman.

In the middle of New York's Chinatown there is a three-story brick building with the sign "E. VOGEL, Custom Made Shoes & Boots since 1879." The "E" stands for Egidius, the first name of the German immigrant who caused so much excitement with his new shoe designs, which were regarded as revolutionary at the time. The winged toe caps of his shoes really did have more extravagant curves than those of other manufacturers.

Of course, every famous shoemaker seeks to offer their customers the widest possible selection of shoes and designs. A bespoke shoe from the E. Vogel collection is particularly easy to pick out: the customer's name is handwritten on the leather lining of the shoe. This is important for identification purposes, but is also a sign of attention to detail.

In this friendly interior at the workshop of Oliver Moore the company's employees initiate their customers into the secrets of perfect shoemaking. This is where measurements are taken, and designs and materials are selected. The next time the customer comes to this room is for the final fitting session.

These Shoes are Made for Walking: Oliver Moore in New York

Oliver Moore are responsible for some of the most beautiful handmade shoes in New York. The current owner is Elisabeth Moore, the widow of Thomas Moore, the grandson of the firm's founder.

The eponymous founder of the firm, Oliver Moore, learned the craft of shoemaking in England, and took his knowledge and love of tradition with him to the USA in 1878. Since that time Moore have counted many famous personalities among their customers, including Theodore Roosevelt, George Raft, and Leonard Lauder.

On account of the high quality of the company's bespoke shoes, the workshop serves many regular customers who have their own lasts in store at Moore and are able to order new shoes direct by telephone, which is useful if they are unable to visit New York.

A young shoemaker needs five or six years' professional experience before he can make a perfect Oliver Moore full-brogue Oxford, so he will need to be patient to learn the craft well.

Glossary

A

Addition method

A method of fitting up the custom-made last. If the foot is broader, the instep or big toe higher, or the heel thicker than the average, the shoemaker corrects the last by attaching various pieces of leather to it. Though the shoemaker can use this corrected last to make the shoe, it is advisable to produce a definitive last by fine copying it.

Ankle boots

Footwear for colder days, with sides reaching 2–4 inches [5–10 cm] above the ankle bone and fastened with eyelets, hooks, or buttons. Their doubled soles give the feet extra protection.

Arch supports

At an early stage, fallen arches can be counteracted with supports. This is why it is important for the shoemaker to form a precise idea of the state of the arches.

Awl

The shoemaker uses a long awl to make holes in the welt for the stitches and a short one to make the holes for the wooden pegs in the rand.

Awl holes

Square holes made with the awl for the wooden pegs used to attach the rand. The holes are eventually sealed with adhesive.

B

Back stiffener

A leather reinforcement inside the shoe at the point where the quarters meet.

Basic forme

Used to produce the design for the upper. The designer transfers the design from the last onto paper.

Bend leather

The most valuable, hardest, and most massive part of a cowhide, between one-fifth and one-third of an inch [5–8 mm] thick, water and temperature resistant and easy to work, that has been softened and stored in the tanning pits for at least 15–18 months. It is used for the top sole and the heel (both the lifts and the top piece).

Box calf

Calfskin tanned with chrome salts. It is considered to be the best material for shoe uppers and boot legs.

Box cowhide

Cowhide tanned with chrome salts. It is used for shoe uppers.

Breasting iron

A tool with different cross-section sizes used by the shoemaker to smooth the edges of the sole and heel and make the material more dense.

Brogueing row

An arrangement of holes of the same or different sizes at regular intervals along the lines and curves where the upper components meet.

Budapest

A well-known full-brogue Derby style of shoe with a high toe cap.

Burnishing iron

Iron tool that the shoemaker heats to the required temperature over a flame and uses to press ink and shoe cream into the leather.

C

Cleaning brush

A coarse brush for removing dirt, made of pig bristles, the tailhair of cattle or horses, or agave fibers.

Clicking

Cutting out the upper components from the appropriate leather in accordance with the style formes.

Closing

Sewing the upper components together with single or double rows of stitches, depending on the strain to which the components will be exposed.

Closing shop

The workshop where the upper components were traditionally reinforced and stitched together. Today uppers are made industrially and supplied to the shoemaker.

Cobbler's hammer

Weighing some 18 ounces [500 g], the cobbler's hammer is similar to a household hammer – and has many uses.

Collar

A thin, rolled strip of leather serving to reinforce and decorate the upper areas of the quarters.

Cordovan

Horsehide tanned with chrome salts. It is used for shoe uppers and boot legs.

Cowhide

The raw material for shoe manufacture. The strongest and most massive part of the hide is located on either side of the spinal column. The neck section is used for the insole and middle sole, the belly for the welt, heel cup, and vamp. Vegetable-tanned leather is suitable for the lining and the lower parts of the shoe, chemical-tanned leather for the upper (see also bend leather).

Custom-made lasts

See last.

Custom-made shoes

Handmade shoes that fit the feet perfectly. They are manufactured on the basis of the information gathered in the measurement-taking process.

D

Decorative pattern

A perforated design, usually geometric, on the vamp. Typical of the full-brogue and semi-brogue types.

Derby

An open-laced style of shoe widespread in Europe, often double stitched and double soled. Also known as "Bluchers." The most common variants are plain, full-brogues, and semi-brogues.

Direction of stretch

The direction of stretch of the upper leather is important to the placing of the formes. The forme for the vamp, for example, must be oriented so that the leather can expand lengthwise but not across – whereas if the quarters can expand lengthwise, they will stretch by two-fifths to four-fifths of an inch [1–2 cm] and the shoe will lose its shape and fit.

Double-stitched shoe

A handmade shoe with one sole and two stitch rows, or two soles and three stitch rows. All the stitch rows are externally visible. A strong, casual type of shoe. There are two very common variants of the double-stitched shoe: in the first the welt runs from one edge of the heel to the other, in the second the welt also embraces the heel – in which case the heel area is wider than usual. A strong, smooth leather is suitable for double-stitched shoes, or one with a rough surface; combinations of different colors are also frequent. Variants covering the ankles are very popular, as are boots.

E

Eyelets

Holes one-eighth to one-twelfth of an inch [2–3 mm] across at intervals of two-fifths to three-fifths of an inch [1–1.5 cm] through which the shoe laces are threaded. Classic gentlemen's shoes normally have five pairs of eyelets.

F

Filling

Substance used to fill the gap in a welt-stitched shoe, with a shock-absorbing and stabilizing effect on the sole when walking.

Fine copying

1. Lastmaking method in which the measurements of the last forme are precisely transferred to the new last by machine.
2. Lastmaking method in which a last that has been corrected by the addition method functions as a last forme.

Finishing

The final process undergone by the shoe once its construction is complete, consisting of washing, creaming, and polishing the upper; and inking, heelballing, and polishing the edges of the sole and the heel. The edge of the sole is pressed with the edge iron and the edges of the heel smoothed with the dummy iron, and both are then individually patterned with the fancy wheels. The top piece and sole are creamed or inked.

Finishing wax

Type of wax, of which the shoemaker applies a thin coat to the upper surfaces of the shoe after inking. It is then pressed into the leather together with the ink using a warm iron.

Foot arch

The lengthwise and transverse arch of the foot. It bears the entire body weight when standing and walking. It acts as a shock absorber, reducing the impact on the head and spinal column of walking.

Foot documentation

All the important information about the feet and their owner established in the measurement-taking process: the measurement record, foot imprint, draft drawings, and marked-up lasts.

Foot elevation

The side and rear elevation of the foot transferred onto paper.

Foot imprint

An imprint of the foot produced by the Ped-a-graph. It gives an exact picture of the arch of the foot, the intersection points of the arch curves, and the position of the toes.

Foot outline

The shoemaker makes an outline of the foot with a vertically held pencil on a sheet of paper, from which the length and width of the shoes are then measured.

Full-brogue

A type of shoe decorated with perforated patterns, with winged toe caps and rows of perforations.

G

Gimping

Trimming and simultaneously decorating the edges of leather pieces. The shoemaker does this with a gimping machine in which steel tools with various patterns and designs can be fitted.

Girths

Characteristic measurements for the individual foot. The girth is measured at the metatarsals, the instep, the heel, and the ankle.

Golfing shoes

Sports shoes that are often handmade. The top sole is fitted with nine to eleven spikes for increased stability on grass-covered ground.

Gouge

Iron tool used to form the feather in the insole.

Grain

The upper layer of the leather is the grain layer. It has hair shafts and the excretory ducts of the sebaceous and sweat glands running through it; these give it its "grain." Every leather possesses its own characteristic grain.

H

Half-brogue

See semi-brogue.

Hand-stitched shoe

A shoe made by the traditional method. The two most important types of hand-stitched shoe are the welt-stitched and double-stitched variants.

Heel

Structure consisting of a number of leather lifts and acting as a support while walking. Four to six lifts are needed for the heel of a gentleman's shoe. Two inches [5 cm] is the ideal height.

Heel construction

Several leather lifts, a top piece, and a quarter rubber are assembled to form the heel.

Heel cup

A piece of leather (part of the upper) on the outside of the back of the shoe covering the seam joining the quarters. It may be a narrow strip or a long, vertical piece of leather in line with the heel.

Heel edge

The outer surface of the heel. Usually it is black, but sometimes it is colored to match the upper leather. If it is not colored, the individual lifts are readily discernible.

Heel lifts

Two to four pieces of leather cut to the shape of the heel, which they jointly form.

Heel section

The back of the shoe.

I

Inner sock

Leather lining in direct contact with the foot. The customer can specify that it should cover the whole of the insole, three-quarters of it, or only a quarter (under the heel).

Insole

The foundation of the shoe: a piece of leather between one-tenth and one-seventh of an inch [2.5–3.5 mm] thick, depending on the robustness of the shoe, on which the shoe is built. The initial stage is to nail the insole to the last. A feather is then formed with the gouge.

L

Lacing

Horizontal lacing, characteristic of the Oxford, is more elegant – while crossover lacing is more casual, characteristic of the Derby. It can be varied individually, however.

Last

A wooden instrument used for making shoes. Its shape and dimensions represent the customer's foot and the required type of shoe in abstract form.
1. Asymmetric lasts: the two lasts are different, reflecting the left and right feet; in use in ancient times and again from the beginning of the nineteenth century.
2. Symmetric lasts: measurements of only one foot were taken and used for both lasts; in use from the fifteenth century until the end of the eighteenth; customers always had difficulty breaking in shoes made on them.

3. Custom-made lasts: produced using all the foot documentation and thus reflecting every characteristic feature of the individual feet and the type of last.

Last removal

The removal of the last from the completed shoe. The shoemaker carefully pulls it out using the foot strap and an iron hook about a quarter inch [6–7 mm] thick, adjusting the pressure with the foot strap.

Last type

This determines the shape of the shoe. The differences lie in the shape and width of the vamp. It is the responsibility of the shoemaker to obtain the right type of last for his client.

Lasting

Nailing the upper to the insole on the last. The last now gives the upper a plastic form.

Lining leather

Vegetable-tanned leather on average one-twentieth of an inch [1.2 mm] thick, used to line the inside of the shoe. Though especially soft, it is also hard wearing.

Loafer

See slip-on.

M

Mark

A cut made in the top sole for the top-sole seam.

Measurement taking

The recording of the most important data relating to the foot in order to draw up the necessary foot documentation. It should take place at a time when the feet are in an ideal state. The measurement-taking process has a ceremonial character.

Middle sole

A sole between the welt and the top sole. Characteristic of double-soled shoes.

Middle-sole seam

The seam holding the welt and the middle sole together.

Monk

A puritanical-looking shoe, as its name suggests. Its most striking feature is the fact that its quarters are fastened together with a buckle, or even two, and it is often richly decorated. It owes its elegance to its long vamp.

N

Norwegian shoe

A variant of the basic Derby, a controversial, flamboyant, and youthful style characterized by an unusual division of the vamp and hand stitching on the upper. Its rustic character is often accentuated with heavily grained leather.

O

Oxford

An esthetically elegant style with closed lacing. It typically comes in plain, full-brogue, and semi-brogue versions.

P

Paste

A mixture prepared by combining wheat starch, pieces of dried chestnut or potato, and water. It has a stiffening as well as a strengthening effect.

Penny Loafer

See slip-on.

Plain

A style in which the vamp is not subdivided or perforated.

Putting-on brushes

Brushes made of soft horsehair, used to apply shoe cream; it is advisable to use a separate brush for each color.

Q

Quarter

Part of the upper. The two quarters cover the inner and outer sides of the foot, reaching from the instep to the back of the heel (where they meet). The height of the quarters at the inside of the ankle bone is 2 inches [5 cm] in shoes and an additional 2–4 inches [5–10 cm] in ankle boots.

Quarter rubber

A piece of hard, non-slip rubber a quarter inch [6 mm] thick that is nailed to the top piece of the heel.

R

Rand

1. A leather strip four-fifths of an inch [2 cm] wide and one-eighth of an inch [3 mm] thick that is nailed onto the insole, combining with the welt to form a basis for the top sole.
2. A special welt in the heel region, nailed in a welt-stitched shoe and stitched in a double-stitched model.

Rawhide

A skin cleaned and ready for tanning.

Raw hides

Untreated animal skins.

Removal method

A method of fitting up the custom-made last. If the foot is narrower or the instep flatter than the average, the shoemaker removes the excess wood from the last – in other words, he takes material away.

Repair service

Any good shoemaking workshop offers its customers a repair service. It is important for it to be used regularly in order to give the shoes a long life.

Rough copying

The measurements are roughly transferred from the forme to a block of wood by machine, thus forming the rough last.

Rubber solution
Rubber dissolved in benzene. This sort of adhesive dries within ten to fifteen minutes and remains flexible and resilient when dry.

S
Sandal
A shoe style of Greek origin, now purely a summer shoe.

Sandpaper
Paper with a rough surface, from coarse to fine, used to smooth edges.

Scotch grain
A variant of box cowhide with a surface that is not smooth, but has had a pattern burned into it at high temperature. Whole uppers are made of Scotch grain, but it is also suitable for combination with other leathers.

Screw stretcher
A device for widening the shoe by hand.

Semi-brogue
A shoe style with perforated decoration, a plain toe cap, and brogueing rows. Also known as half-brogue.

Sewing thread
Cotton or strong linen thread. Silk is recommended for stitching very delicate upper components together. Sewing thread for the uppers consists of three, four, six, or nine strands. The fineness of a thread is a function of its length in meters and its weight in grams. The color of the thread should be one shade darker than the color of the upper leather.

Shank
A steel spring some 4 inches [10 cm] long and three-fifths of an inch [1.5 cm] wide that strengthens the region of the waist in the gap formed by the welt and the insole. It stiffens this part of the shoe, which must not move when walking.

Shoe assembly
The working phase of shoe production in which the insole is nailed to the last and attached to the edge of the upper, the welt and the top sole are sewn on, and the heel is built.

Shoe-care set
Every owner of handmade shoes should possess a shoe-care set consisting of cleaning brush, putting-on brushes, creams, cloths, and polishing brushes so he can take proper care of his shoes.

Shoe horn
A guiding implement made of wood, horn, or metal that covers and stiffens the back of the shoe while the foot slips into it. Shorter shoe horns are suitable for shoes, longer ones for boots and ankle boots.

Shoemaker's knife
A steel knife with a slightly curved blade, used for cutting out the lower parts of the shoe (sole, heel lifts), a quarter to a third of an inch [6–8 mm] thick.

Shoemaker's tape measure
A nonelastic textile strip calibrated in French stitches on one side and metric units on the other.

Shoe style
A shoe with the special form and esthetic features of a particular style. The customer selects the style in which he wishes his custom-made shoes to be produced.

Shoe trees
Pieces of wood shaped like a last, designed to keep the shoes in shape. The two most frequent and popular designs are the three-piece shoe tree and the sprung shoe tree.

Side linings
Narrow pieces of leather cut from the same hide as the upper leather and placed between the upper and lining leathers and between the toe cap and the heel cup to stop the leather stretching and to strengthen both sides of the shoe.

Size
A number indicating the length of the shoe. Various measuring systems are in use: French, English, American, and metric.

Skiver
A small, sharp plane with a guide channel in it used to remove any protruding surfaces of leather, fraction by fraction, and to match up the edges of sole and heel.

Slip-on
A shoe style with no laces or buckles, into which the wearer simply slips his foot (also called a loafer). Its forebear is the Indian moccasin. Today slip-ons also exist in welt-stitched form. One of these is the Penny Loafer, where the tongue is covered by a leather cross-strap under which wearers used to place a one-penny coin.

Sole
A component in the lower part of the shoe. Single-soled shoes have only a top sole, which makes contact with the ground. Double-soled shoes have a top sole and a middle sole.

Sole edge
The edge of the welt and the top sole or of the welt, middle sole, and top sole.

Sole leather
See bend leather.

Soling
1. The process of sticking and sewing the top sole cut out of bend leather to the welt.
2. Fitting a new sole to shoes handed in for repair.

Steel plate
Often used instead of a quarter rubber to give a better grip on slippery surfaces.

Stiffeners
Pieces of leather cut from the same hide as the upper leather that are placed beneath brogueing rows, for example, or on the upper part of the tongue.

Stitching-channel flap
The leather edge formed when material is pared away from the mark. It covers the top-sole seam, which would otherwise make contact with the ground and quickly get worn away, sooner or later leading to the separation of the sole.

Stretcher
A metal device for widening the shoe.

Style collection
A collection of shoe styles in the showrooms of the shoemaking workshop.

Style design
A drawing of the shoe to be made, with its decoration, seams, and the shapes of the individual components, on the last itself. This enables the design to be examined in three dimensions.

Style designer
The style designer, on the basis of classical traditions, designs the shape and decoration of the upper, the proportions of its components, varies colors and materials, and creates new combinations. He constantly attempts to add new elements to the classical traditions.

Style form
A form for the upper components. It highlights where the components meet, their relative size, and all lines, curves, and decorations. It is used to make individual forms for the upper components.

T

Taking-off brushes
Brushes for polishing, made of the tail or mane hair of the horse. A separate brush should be used for each color.

Tanning
The treatment of skin with tanning agents to render it durable, resilient, hard-wearing, and soft. There are two main types of tanning.
1. Vegetable tanning, in which skins are tanned in pits with plant extracts such as spruce, oak, or alder wood; oak galls, pomegranates, or acorn seed husks. It is mainly the lower parts of the shoe that undergo vegetable tanning.
2. Mineral tanning, in which skins are tanned in drums with alum or chromium salts, the latter shortening the otherwise protracted tanning period to six or seven weeks. It is mainly the upper leather that undergoes mineral tanning.

Tanning pits (pit tanning)
Lined oak or cement pits for vegetable tanning. Layers of skins are placed in the pit – alternating with plant extracts – submerged in tanning liquor, and left to soften for a certain period of time.

Toe cap
1. Internal: leather stiffener at the tip of the shoe. It is used in shoes with a one-piece upper, in which case it is not immediately apparent whether the shoe was made with or without a toe cap. If the vamp is divided, the toe cap can have a straight (semi-brogue) or winged (full-brogue) shape.
2. External: that part of the upper that corresponds in shape to the internal toe cap.

Tongue
A leather flap attached to the inside or outside of the upper to protect the lacing area from friction, pressure, and penetration by extraneous objects. It also often functions as a decorative component.

Top piece
The lift of the heel that is in direct contact with the ground.

Top-sole seam
This seam joins the welt to the top sole (in single-soled shoes) and to the middle and top soles (in double-soled shoes).

Trial shoe
A shoe made in medium-quality leather on the custom-made last. If the trial shoe is a poor fit in places, corrections can be made to the last.

U

Upper
The topmost part of the shoe. Depending on the shoe type and style, it consists of one or more components: the toe cap, vamp, tongue, quarters, and back.

Upper features
Items that either reinforce or decorate the upper: linen lining, eyelet facing with underlay, collar, lining leather.

Upper leather
Leather from the highest-quality layer of the hide, tanned with chrome salts. It is used to make the upper. Upper leather is normally between one-fifteenth and one-twentieth of an inch [1.2–1.5 mm] thick.

Upper reinforcers
Leather or textile stiffeners for those regions of the upper where the danger of stretching is greatest.

V

Vamp
The front of the shoe, consisting of one piece (in the slip-on) or several (toe cap, vamp insertion). Its shape depends on the shoe style.

W

Welt
This strip of leather, an average of 24 inches [60 cm] long, four-fifths of an inch [2 cm] wide, and one-eighth of an inch [3 mm] thick, is the foundation of the shoe. It holds the upper, insole, and sole together.

Welt needles
Curved needles just over 3 inches long [8 cm]. Two of them are needed for the welt-stitching process.

Welt seam
The seam that holds the upper, insole, and welt together.

Welt-stitched shoe
An elegant, handmade shoe. The welt seam that holds the upper and the insole together is not externally visible. The top-sole seam, which is visible, holds together the welt and the top sole (in a single-soled shoe); or the welt, the middle sole, and the top sole (in double-soled shoes).

Width numbering
This system has 5 to 8 girth measurements. Given the shoe size and width number, the girth at the metatarsals, instep, heel, and ankle can be calculated.

Wing cap
Heart-shaped toe cap. The elegant line extends along the vamp almost as far as the heel.

Further Literature

Andritzky, M., Kämpf, G., Link, V. (eds): Z.B. Schuhe, Giessen 1995

Asensio, F. (ed.): The Best Shops, Barcelona 1990

Bally Schuhmuseum (ed.): 'Graphik rund um den Schuh', in: Schriften des Bally Schuhmuseums, Schönenwend 1968

Baynes, K. and K. (eds): The Shoe Show. British Shoes since 1790, London 1979

Blum, S.: Everyday Fashions of the Thirties as Pictured in Sears Catalogs, New York 1986

Broby-Johansen, R.: Krop og klaer, Copenhagen 1966

Deutsches Ledermuseum (ed.): Catalog, vol. 6, Offenbach 1980

Durain-Ress, S.: Schuhe. Vom späten Mittelalter bis zur Gegenwart, Munich 1991

McDowell, C.: Schuhe, Schönheit – Mode – Phantasie, Munich 1989

Fehér , Gy., Szunyoghy, A.: Zeichenschule, Cologne 1996

Flórán, M.: Tanners. The Tannery from Baja in the Hungarian Open Air Museum, Szentendre 1992

Friedrich, R.: Leder, Gestalten und Verarbeiten, Munich 1988

Giglinger, K.: Schuh und Leder, Vienna 1990

Gillespie, C.C.: Diderot Pictorial Encyclopedia of Trades and Industry. Manufacturing and Technical Arts in Plates, New York 1993

Geisler, R.: Wie erkenne ich an Leder das Gute und das Mindergute?, Kassel 1949

Göpfrich.: Römische Lederfunde aus Mainz, Offenbach 1986

Hálová-Jahodová, C.: Vergessene Handwerkskunst, Prague 1995

Haufe, G.: Das Zeichnen und Modellieren des Maßschumachers, Leipzig 1954

Honnef, K., Schlüter, B., Küchels, B. (eds): Die verlassenen Schuhe, Bonn 1994

Lubig, E. et al. (eds): Lexikon der Schuhtechnik, Leipzig 1983

L.V.M.H. (ed.): Berlutti, History of a Family of Artists, Paris 1997

Meier, E.: Von Schuhen – Eine Fibel, Munich 1994

The Museum of Leathercraft (ed.): A Picture Book of Leather, London 1959

O'Keeffe, L.: Schuhe, Cologne 1997

Probert, C.: Shoes in Vogue since 1910, London 1981

The Swenters Shoe Art: Shoes or no Shoes, Antwerp 1997

Vorwold, W., Dittmar, K.: Fachkunde für Schuhmacher, Wiesbaden 1952

Weber, P.: Der Schuhmacher. Ein Beruf im Wandel der Zeit, Stuttgart 1988

Weber, P.: Schuhe, Drei Jahrtausende in Bildern, Stuttgart 1986

Workshop Catalogs and Periodicals

Allen Edmonds' Workshop Catalog, spring collection 1997

Cheaney's Workshop Catalog, 1997

Edition Schuhe, Düsseldorf (half yearly from 1996)

Edition Schuhe: Rahmengenähte Herrenschuhe, Düsseldorf, 1997

John Spencer's Workshop Catalog, 1997

John Lobb's Workshop Catalog, 1998

Ludwig Reiter's Workshop Catalog, 1996

Dunkelmann and Son's Workshop Catalog, 1998

Grenson Shoes' Workshop Catalog, 1998

Church's Workshop Catalog, 1997

Himer & Himer Workshop Catalog, 1998

Krisam und Wittling's Workshop Catalog of custom-made shoes, 1998

Joh. Rendenbach's Workshop Catalog, 1998

STEP. Schuhe, Leder, Accessoires, Düsseldorf Nov./Dec. 1996

Tanneries du Puy Workshop Catalog, 1998

Vogel's Workshop Catalog, 1998

Acknowledgments

The authors express their gratitude to the following for their patient supply of information, their expert advice, their enlightening conversations, and the diverse support they have provided.

In the László Vass workshop, Budapest:
Ottó Lang (designer); György Szkala, Györgyné Szkala (clickers); Józsefné Süle (chief craftsman, closing workshop); Bertalanné Szabó, Istvánné Simon, Dóra Gaál (closers); Ferenc Varga (master craftsman); László Kovács, Károly Kardos, Dénes Bíró, Sándor Kocsis, Albert Szabó, Árpád Ungvári, Ferenc Juhász, Dénes Mihály, Bálint Dobai, Dénes Boga, Csaba Nemes, János Soltész, József Zatyi (shoemakers); Attiláné Turcsányi, Eniki Cserhalmi, Andrea Élias (finishers); Róbert Magyar, György Haris (models).

The authors and publishers also wish to thank the following firms and institutions for their friendly support:

Joh. Rendenbach company (Altgerber Verband e.V., Trier); János Csillag (Pécsi Bőrgyár Rt., Pécs); István Gál (Finombőrgyártó Rt., Budapest); Kálmán Berta and Kálmán Berta junior (lastmakers, Pápa); the Offenbach Leather Museum; Fritz Minke company (leather and orthopedic wholesalers, Duisburg); Silke Dworak-Schneider and Manfred Schneider (master orthopedic shoemakers, Kiel); Helfried Trost (shoemaker and master orthopedic shoemaker, Offenbach); Zoltán Nagy (Shoe Museum, Körmend); Lajos Bálint (workshop, Vienna); Axel Himer (workshop, Baden-Baden); Jack Lynch (E. Vogel workshop, New York); John Hunter Lobb (workshop, London); Paul Moorefield (Moore workshop, New York); Benjamin Klemann (workshop, Basthorst).

The photographer wishes to thank:
Umberto Angeloni, Brioni, SpA; Oliver Bialowons; Edward's, Cologne; Albert Kreca; Macho company, Vienna; Peter von Quadt; and, for their photographic collaboration and assistance: Imke Jungjohann; Zoltán Miklóska; Holger Rogge; Peter Somalvi (photographic assistants, Cologne and Budapest); Ruprecht Stempell (photographic studio, Cologne).

The publishers also wish to thank Bernhard Roetzel for acting as consultant.

Index

Illustrations

The overwhelming majority of the illustrations, which are not individually listed here, are new photographs taken by Cologne photographer Georg Valerius. Prior to going to press the editors and publishers made intensive efforts to locate all other holders of illustration rights. Persons and institutions holding such rights to illustrations used who may not have been contacted are requested to contact the publishers.